ALVIS CARS IN COMPETITION

CLIVE TAYLOR

This book is dedicated to Brian Maile, who had been my sole confidant and UK contact in the early stages of planning and preparing this book, and latterly to Charles Mackonochie, for handling owners' precious photographs, in liaison with our publisher Amberley Publishing.

Owners both past and present throughout the world owe a great debt of gratitude for the pleasure they have derived from their Alvis to T. G. John, the founder and innovator of the Alvis marque.

Front Cover: *En-route to Darwin from Melbourne, stopping at Uluru (previously Ayers Rock) in southern Northern Territory, Australia. (Rüdi Friedrichs)*

Back Cover: *Top to bottom: Brian Chant competes in* Brutus, *a 4.3 Alvis, at Gurston Down Hillclimb in 1984 (Brian Chant Collection); Rüdi Friedrichs racing his 4.3 in Europe, ahead of a Morgan and Bugattis (Rüdi Friedrichs Collection); our Alvis Firefly resting in the Clare Valley, South Australia, in 1999 (Dale Parsell); Alvis front-wheel drive overlooking the hills of Howrah, the River Derwent and the distant Hobart Hills. (Mike Williams)*

First published 2018

Amberley Publishing
The Hill, Stroud
Gloucestershire, GL5 4EP

www.amberley-books.com

British Library Cataloguing in Publication Data.
A catalogue record for this book is available from the British Library.

ISBN 978 1 4456 7516 9 (print)
ISBN 978 1 4456 7517 6 (ebook)

Origination by Amberley Publishing.
Printed in Great Britain.

FOREWORD

The purpose and scope of this book is to celebrate and recognise the forthcoming centenary in 2019 of the Alvis Car Company by illustrating a variety of cars used in various types of competition by their owners. I am grateful to all the contributors herein, who responded to the published invitations to be involved and for their willingness to share their unique story about their Alvis car and how they use it in various forms of competition. Without their positive contributions, the format and content of this book would not have been possible.

In the early years, from 1920 to the mid-1930s, Alvis produced cars used for racing, hillclimbing and long-distance road trials for publicity purposes to good effect. Due to increasing costs they stopped official works entries and competition was then the province of wealthy owners, who pursued their own endeavours for the Alvis marque until the Second World War.

Post-war, the new models Alvis produced were mainly used for road rallies and timed trials, such as the RAC rallies and the Monte Carlo Rally. For track racing, hillclimbs, sprints, trials and period historic rallies, owners have used mainly pre-war cars and have also used pre-war parts to build what are now known as Specials, as you will read in the stories that follow, which can be seen competing in current historic competitive events around the world.

It is a well-known fact that an Alvis properly prepared can undertake and complete any form of competition without incurring any problems. Alvis cars excel in the current popular long-distance events such as the Peking to Paris Rally, LeJog (Land's End to John O' Groats), The Flying Scotsman Vintage Rally, the 1,000 Mile Trial and the Samurai Rally, as well as crossing Australia and Africa, and many more kindred events.

For those of you reading this book who do not own an Alvis, you will find all the current Alvis Car Club contacts at the back of this book for your encouragement to do so, together with a detailed bibliography about the marque. Owning and using an Alvis will change your life for the better, as the stories within this book will testify.

Clive Taylor
Tauranga, New Zealand

VINTAGE PERIOD: 1919 TO 1931

Car Details: 1923 12/40 with 12/50 Cylinder Head; Registration No. ND 2345; Chassis No. 2053; Engine No. 2411; Car No. 7390; Body Maker – Cubitt Engineering.

I first acquired ND in 1968 from Peter Harper of Stretton, near Warrington, Cheshire. ND had been rescued from a twenty-five-year slumber by Peter's brother, Michael. I paid the princely sum of £750 for her and drove home to Albrighton on a very foggy day, with two red bicycle lamps tied on the rear as those on ND did not work.

The top end was overhauled and we generally went through the car to make it reliable and roadworthy. After a few enjoyable runs I sold ND to George Bolam of Moreton-in-Marsh and immediately regretted it.

Two years later I bought it back off George, who had changed the colour from ivory with black wings to blue with black wings. He had also re-trimmed the car and had the engine rebuilt by Nigel Arnold-Forster.

Over the next decade ND was used for holidays to the Isle of Wight, Wales and Cornwall. The car also competed in numerous motor sport events including races, hillclimbs, sprints, rallies and trials.

Among the more notable events were the 1974 Richard Seaman Trophy Race at Oulton Park on June 15, the July 1974 VSCC Silverstone meeting, and the 1977 Itala Trophy meeting, which was also at Silverstone. ND always ran faultlessly, although it was usually given a tough handicap for a standard five-seater, artillery-wheeled tourer.

The car also won the best Alvis on handicap and the 12/50 Trophy at the Curborough Sprint in 1979. In 1980 it won the Alvis Owner Club Midland Trophy, as well as the 12/50 Trophy. ND also took part in the VSCC Wessex Trial and the Welsh Rally.

On the latter event, I broke the differential and spent the afternoon in Presteigne High Street, removing the crown wheel and pinion only to find that the spare one, which a friend had brought to Presteigne for me, did not fit. The homeward journey was by trailer, and was the only time ND failed to get me home under her own power. On one occasion, when Steve Denner was visiting the UK from Australia, he borrowed ND to compete at the VSCC Shelsley Walsh Hillclimb.

I parted with ND in 1985, part exchanging the old girl for an XK 120 roadster. Throughout my ownership I maintained ND myself and found it a delight to work on. The car originally started life as a 12/40 but was brought up to 12/50 spec at the works by the addition of an overhead valve cylinder head and a braked front axle. She still had the original cone clutch, belt driven dynamo and twin rear brake shoes.

I chose to run a sports Alvis when I was seventeen because my friend Rob Jones had a 12/60 tourer and the quality and performance really impressed me. ND certainly lived up to my expectations, and is now owned by Alan Eatwell, who is currently treating her to another comprehensive rebuild.

Mike Ridley

At high speed coming around
Woodcote Corner at Silverstone as
No. 164 on 16 April 1977. (Photograph
Harold Barker)

Racing at Oulton Park in June 1974,
No. 169 is ahead of the Amilcar.
(Photograph Roger McDonald)

Racing at the VSCC July Silverstone
1974, No. 170. (Photograph
Jane Rushden)

ALVIS CARS IN COMPETITION

Car Details: 1924 SC 12/50; Registration No. OO NSW 372; Chassis No. 3390; Engine No. 3751; Body Maker – Carbodies. Nicknamed Naked Norah after a scantily dressed barmaid.

Alvis despatched this car in 1924 and delivered it to Regent Motors, St Kilda, Melbourne. The first owner, Cyril Ambler, a local grain merchant, bought the car in 1925, eventually trading the car for a Speed 20 with Regent Motors.

Gerald S. Wardell, who was an engineer in Ballarat, bought the car in 1934. At some point he rolled the car landing in a culvert. The damaged aluminium panel had to be replaced in steel due to a shortage of aluminium and he painted the car pea green in memory of Phil Garlick, who had raced Alvis cars in the past. During Gerald's ownership, a rear brake drum burst, and Lysaghts, in Port Kembla, made a new set. Gerald sold the car in 1949 to Alvis agents Charley & Lord. The third owner, Geoff Goodman, only had the car for a short time, selling it to buy a Mercedes-Benz.

The fourth owner is not recorded, and Mr Doyle became the fifth owner. When Bill Boldiston saw the advert to sell in 1949, he met Mr Doyle, paid his £10 deposit and borrowed the balance of £110 and brought Norah home. The colour was changed to 'Alvis colours' – dark blue and dove grey. As there was some discontent about competition events at the time, Bill became involved in establishing the Alvis Car Club, organising hillclimbs and sprints and so on. This Club was formed on 28 September 1950 in his home in Willoughby and he was elected the first Club Secretary, with Norm Adams as President.

In 1952 Bill was transferred to Newcastle, returning to Sydney at weekends, with the Alvis clocking up 10,000 miles a year just taking him to work! He married in 1955, and used the car to carry equipment to build his home in Forestville. 'Big Foot' tyres were fitted to make the ride more comfortable for his honeymoon in Melbourne. On their return, the car was entered into the Club's first Mt Druitt Petit Prix, sprinting up and down the airstrip.

By 1956 Bill was working in the Rydalmere area on a new telephone exchange, drawing Regulation 90 fuel for on-site inspections. As his family grew, the car had a sojourn for a few years. Historic racing began to emerge and Bill wanted to compete again, and Norm Adams repainted the car in colours similar to those used by Gerry Wardell. In 1978 the Victorian VSCC celebrated the first Australian Grand Prix on Phillip Island and Norah was entered into this event. During 1988 the Australian Veteran Car Club organised a 'Round Australia Rally' and, as No. 222, Norah participated into the NSW and ACT (Australian Capital Territory) areas.

When Bill retired he bought the disused Medlow Bath Post Office building and renovated it, housing Norah. Bill organised the Early Morning Soup Run from Parramatta, starting at 7.00 a.m. and finishing at the Old Post Office, which became an annual event. With the help of the Confederation of Australian Motor Sport (CAMS), the local Catalina Park circuit was activated again with an annual event called the Bol D'Or. In 1978 he met Joe Wilson at Oran Park, who eventually bought Bill's Amilcar and later asked if he could buy the Alvis Norah for his son, Andrew.

After sixty years of ownership, he agreed to sell Norah, and she is now in a younger generation's hands with a new future ahead of her. As a matter of interest, Bill has recorded the history of this car in his privately published book When You're On A Good Thing (Sixty Years With the Right Car). Norah is now carefully maintained in the house of the Morris family.

Transcribed by Clive Taylor

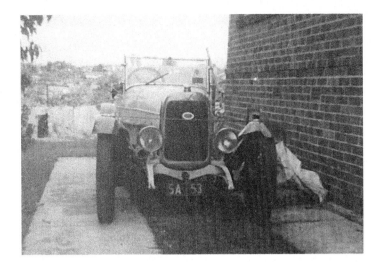

At last, my Alvis arriving at my home in 1949. (Bill Boldiston)

Working at Rydalmere at the temporary telephone exchange in 1959. (Bill Boldiston Collection)

Racing Norah at Amaroo Park in 1981. (Francois Mommaerts)

ALVIS CARS IN COMPETITION

Car Details: 1925 SC 12/50; Registration No. 5 – 329; Chassis No. 3514; Engine No. 3856; Car No. 8801; Body Maker – Body built in Melbourne.

This car was dispatched from the Alvis works in chassis form (with optional front wheel brakes) on 6 April 1925 to Messrs. Tozer, Kemsley & Millbourne of London, and was one of a batch of forty-nine 12/40s and 12/50s shipped to Melbourne that year.

First registered in Melbourne in 1932, it had been fitted with a locally built four-seat sports tourer body. After some twenty-four years, three or four owners, and suffering the indignity of being converted to a delivery van, it was purchased by Paul Conrad, who removed the body and used the chassis as the basis for a vintage racing car. Between 1956 and 1988 Paul competed with the car, first as a bare chassis, then later in its racing career with a body that had been removed from another 12/50. During this time it underwent continuous development, including lightening by means of extensive drilling of the chassis, brake drums, clutch and brake levers, handbrake lever and even the Hartford shock-absorber arms. It was shortened to 96 inches, with the radiator engine and transmission moved rearwards and the car being lowered by 6 inches, with 19-inch wheels being fitted. In the ongoing weight reduction campaign, the front brakes were removed and the rear axle, with its twin brake shoes, was substituted with a lighter 16/95 version, having only single brake shoes. The carburettor was upgraded to a 35 mm barrel throttle Solex.

Right from the start car was very successful in its racing career. This is how 'Austra' reported one of its outings at Rob Roy Hillclimb, near Melbourne, in a VSCC journal in August 1958:

Undoubtedly the hero of the day was Paul Conrad, whose Alvis is fairly standard except for the fact that its wheel base has been slightly shortened and that it runs as a completely naked chassis. Normally such nudity would be an advantage, but on the day the driver had not only to contend with almost solid rain, but also four miniature cyclonic storms of the car's own making so that how he saw his way up the hill at all remains a mystery. This did not prevent him from being one of the stalwarts who took advantage of the four runs allowed, and like most of the others who did so his fourth run was the fastest, although by that time the track was more like a river than a road. The efficient and unspectacular performance of the Alvis gained it the important Trophy, the Vintage handicap, and also fastest time of the day by a vintage car.

In 1988, long-time 12/50 owner Des Donnan bought the car and continued to compete with it, though now the focus was on circuit racing rather than hillclimbing and sprints. To this end Des changed the 4.77 final drive ratio to 4.55 and fitted a replacement braked front axle. A vane supercharger drawing through an SU carburettor was fitted, though this did nothing for the performance – it simply used more fuel.

In the late '90s, after more than forty years of racing, Des decided its competition career was over and it was time it was rebuilt. The holes in the chassis were filled in and the chassis was returned to its original length of 10 feet ' inches. The radiator, engine and gearbox were returned to their original mountings. A new aluminium duck's back body was built, using imported Wilkinson mudguards, and new 21-inch wheels made using original centres. The 16/95 rear axle has since been replaced with the correct twin shoe type.

Today the car is back to fairly original specification, and the performance and handling is exemplary for a car well over ninety years old; it is an absolute pleasure to drive. It really is a tribute to its designer and the men who made it all those years ago.

Peter Miller

An unknown venue in the late 1980s. Note the engine, gearbox and radiator have been moved back. Weight saving holes have been drilled everywhere by Paul Conrad. (Peter Miller Collection)

A current photograph. The chassis is now at the original length, with a relocated engine gearbox and radiator. (Peter Miller)

Another current photograph, showing the replica aluminium duck's back body. (Peter Miller)

ALVIS CARS IN COMPETITION

Car Details: 1926 TE 12/50; Registration No. RW 7329; Chassis No. 4321; Engine No. 9102; Car No. 9690; Body Maker – Carbodies.

When I saw an advertisement in the local evening paper for a 1934 Alvis as a teenager who was mad keen on vintage cars, some tense negotiations followed. The vendor was fine, but I first had to convince my parents! My idea was that I could restore it ready for when I was old enough to drive it, which was still eighteen months off. I expect my parents' idea was that it would keep me out of trouble for years. Needless to say they were closer to the mark, because reassembling a dismantled, incomplete Firebird DHC took well over three years. The car stayed for many years, but all the time I was sorry that it hadn't been a Speed 20...

The SA Speed 20 with the early Cross & Ellis body had always been my beau ideal *because of its lightness and vintage appeal. Eventually the Firebird was sold, to be replaced by the long-awaited SA. It was wonderful in many ways, but was also very imaginative in finding ways to go wrong. After three years of persistence, the decision was made that if its appeal lay in its vintage character, then maybe an actual vintage car was required. Wanting to avoid roadside repairs, and ever mindful of running costs, it had to be a 12/50.*

So it was that RW 7329 became the only old car I have ever bought as a result of careful thought, as opposed to opportunity or whimsy. It was bought from an advertisement in The Automobile from Peter Roberts. A previous owner, Brian Dearden-Briggs, had used it for trials, and that was what Peter had got it for, but he then bought a Chrysler instead.

The car originally had a wide two-seater body, and when it was three months old the first owner, Miss E. V. Watson, achieved second place at the August meeting at Shelsley Walsh. Coincidentally, she lived in the same house that Mr Roberts lived in when he sold the car to me seventy-five years later; a fact of which he was totally unaware. The Beetleback body now on the car came from an SD and was fitted, if not before the war, then immediately afterwards. The original front wings were retained but without their valances.

In the 1950s the car was lightly modified for racing by Harry Ratcliffe, after which it went through the hands of several owners before I bought it in 2001. I have reversed some alterations, such as the increased wheel offset and the antisocial exhaust, but have kept others, like the fold-flat windscreen.

My first impression, having bought the car, was how pleasant it was. Since then a great deal of wear and tear has been removed and every task has made a noticeable improvement in the way it drives, showing how the 12/50 will keep on going even when neglected.

Competition these days is limited to navigation rallies – an activity for which the car is ideally suited.

Mike Webb

Miss E. V. Watson competing at Shelsley Walsh in 1926. At this time the car was less than three months old! (Mike Webb Collection)

Harry Ratcliffe racing at Oulton Park in 1961. He raced the cars in the 1950s and early 1960s. (Mike Webb Collection)

Crossing the ford at the 2010 VSCC Western Rally. (Phil Jones)

ALVIS CARS IN COMPETITION

Car Details: 1927 TG 12/50; Registration No. CF 7634; Chassis No. 5245; Engine No. 5589; Car No. 10557; Body Maker – Carbodies

While an Alvis 12/50 should raise the pulse rate of any vintage car enthusiast, one could be forgiven for thinking that the 'Three Quarter Coupé' version may act as a cure for insomnia. However, a drive to watch the racing at Angoulême in France with a friend, whom I was following in his Type 40 Bugatti, impressed him so much that on his return he added a 12/50 to his stable of cars and bikes!

I've owned the car for six years and she's a versatile beauty. The lady navigator who was getting fed up with climbing over the doorless bodywork of my 1925 Amilcar CS loves it. Well, the Alvis has doors for one thing, as well as those strange windows that work on the same principle as a roller blind, a fully lined hood that one (fit) person can operate single-handedly and, of course, seating for four or five. When I lower all the windows and mahogany frames and put on the rose-tinted glasses it could almost be the '60s again.

The car had originally been owned by a comfortably well-off JP who lived in Suffolk. He bought the Alvis for his wife, but had then used it throughout the war years on his duties for the Ministry of Agriculture.

The next owner had used the Alvis widely in the 1950s. In the latter part of 1951, he had taken part in the VSCC Blubberhouses Trial, and then the following year, 1952, he had driven down to the Pyrenees.

Then like many cars in the '60s it ended up a little tired, but fortunately the late Adrian Lloyd went on to own the car and he researched its history, which can be seen here: http://vintage-car-profiles.com/alvis/. With some help from other members I have supplemented that with some 12/50 maintenance experiences at http://vintage-car-profiles.com/1250-Maintenance/.

Having sold the Amilcar in 2011, I was keen to buy a 12/50 again. As a teenager I'd owned a 12/60 and a 12/50. So, forty years later, I sent a letter to twenty-six owners of sports saloons, DHCs and Three-Quarter Coupés that were in 'A2' condition. I received a 100 per cent response rate to my begging letter – what a splendid bunch of people Alvis owners are!

I took the Alvis to Angoulême in 2012 and to Normandy twice in 2013, as well as to Suffolk, Yorkshire, Hampshire and Oxfordshire (where we drove up Kop Hill) for Alvis Register AGMs, and for just meandering around Kent and Sussex.

In 2013 we took the car up a hillclimb at Lyons-la-Forêt in Normandy, but clutch slip at Chanteloup-les-Vignes rather spoilt that climb. In 2015 I entered the Alvis in Shere Hillclimb, a new event held on public roads in Surrey. It's a 'non-competitive' event, but surely that phrase is a non sequitur to any 12/50 owner?

Bruce Sandeman-Craik

Resting in front of the house of the original owner in 1927. (Bruce Sandeman-Craik Collection)

The VSCC Blubberhouses Trial in England, 1952. (Bruce Sandeman-Craik Collection)

ALVIS CARS IN COMPETITION

Car Details: 1928 Supercharged FE 12/75 FWD 1,500cc; Registration No. CK 9999; Chassis No. 7256 LWB; Engine No. 7670; Car No. 12076; Body Maker – Saloon followed by a TT Replica.

Alvis introduced the FWD as a super sports car to be sold only to experienced drivers for road and competition use. Developed in 1925 to dominate the 200-Mile Brooklands endurance race, the motoring press immediately praised these cars highly, which were successful in competition. At Le Mans, two production blown cars finished sixth and ninth and first in their class. Four cars entered the IOM TT Trophy race of the same year; Leon Cushman's supercharged car was just beaten into second place.

In 1928 the first owner, G. C. U. Brown, raced the car at Brooklands. Documents show it raced in this form in June 1929. The car was sold to a Mr Gue, who also raced it in 1930. However, he stripped the original body off and fitted an open two-seater body, racing it in true Brooklands tradition while wearing a tie and cuff links. Mr Gue's goal was to lap Brooklands at over 100 mph in a 1,500cc car. It is not known if he succeeded, but on one occasion the supercharger exploded and he was covered in burning oil. After a year of hospitalisation, Mr Gue sold the car.

In around 1940, during the Second World War, the chassis was shortened by 18 inches, (ref D. M. R. Adams) and a T.T. style body was fitted. The owner and racing driver Dickie Stoop and Tony Gaze, another racing driver, were stationed at Westhampnett airfield as part of Battle of Britain crack air squadrons. During this period they raced around the perimeter track of the airfield, laying down the foundation for the Goodwood Race Circuit, and it was Tony Gaze who suggested to Freddie, Duke of Richmond, that 'his Westhampnett' would be an ideal replacement for Brooklands after the war!

In the late 1980s the TT-type body, badly dilapidated and discarded, was replaced with a new TT-style body made from Alvis factory plans and dimensions to match exactly the original Alvis body design. This was 'forced' on the owner, John Robson, due to Hurricane Hugo visiting the house where CK 9999 was stored.

A new ash frame was made by Vintage Autos in South Carolina, panel beating and finishing by Automotive Restorations in Stratford, Connecticut, and the aluminium bonnet by Wilkinson's of Derby, England. Cycle-type wings and supports fabricated in England are exact replicas of the original TT body. The steering was completely restored, and brake drums were machined, while new linings, springs, brake cables, pedal rubbers and throttle linkages were made and the steering wheel was restored. The instruments were restored by John Marks, Vintage Restorations. A replica rev. counter was made by Speedograph Richfield, and a replica supercharger pressure gauge came from Renowned Instruments. New wheels were manufactured by Specialised Motor Services of Macclesfield, finished in Alvis Green acrylic lacquer.

The engine was completely rebuilt with a new crankshaft by Allen Crankshafts, new timing gears by CMG and new steel connecting rods from Alvis Register, along with a rebore with new Jahns pistons, valves, springs and guides. New top, side and bottom water hose castings and a transfer plate with the water pump rebuilt were included. An oil pump was reconditioned, and the pick-up modified with double capacity gears. The oil distribution system has been redesigned and the oil supply to No. 1 main and connecting rod bearings (a questionable feature of FWD engines) has been assured. An external bypass oil filter has been fitted with a standard spin-on disposable canister. We found the original honeycomb radiator proved to be inadequate and a high-efficiency modern core was fitted in March 2000 with a new radiator shell made by B&G Radiators.

The electrics have been rewired with fused circuits, dynamo (output 8 amps), starter and magneto being reconditioned with a non-standard outside three-branch exhaust system and a Brooklands silencer fabricated in stainless steel by Rod Jolley, with a Ki-gas starting system being used. The transmission was completely rebuilt and worn parts have been replaced, with new bearings, a 4.55 to 1 crown wheel and pinion (Alvin Register FWD Cox pattern) being fitted, as well as white metal side thrust bearings being used for the transaxle. Clutch forks have been rebuilt, and a selector gate guard has been fitted to prevent accidental simultaneous engagement of two gears. The reverse gear selector fork has an extra shim to reduce the risk of the lever failing that operates the fork and reverse pinion 'out of gear'.

Allen Eden

Mr Gue in his long-chassis Alvis FWD at Brooklands c. 1928–30. (Allen Eden Collection)

The chassis showing IFS, the engine overhaul crankcase and sump components. (Allen Eden)

FWD chassis construction. (Allen Eden)

ALVIS CARS IN COMPETITION

Car Details: 1928 FWD; Chassis No. 7278 scrapped, now No. 7192; Engine No. 7679; Car No. 12096; Body Maker – Cross & Ellis modified by Brooks Mullins?

The car was despatched on 22 December 1928 to Hallams, Birmingham, England. The original colour was black with a full length ivory stripe but it is now white.

The original owner, Brooke Adie, competed in the car in 1929 at Brooklands at Henly's Alvis Day and entered two races, finishing second of twenty-three entrants to Miss C. P. Hunter, ahead of Ruth Urqhuart-Dykes. She won the second race at 78 mph. Hells Confetti Gazette No. 5 referred to her competing in a Brooklands event on 14 June 1929, which was an event for all comers. Miss Adie was obviously a capable competitor so it would be surprising if she did not also participate in other competitions in the car.

The only other owner known to have competed in the car is Les Lee ('50s and '60s). The photograph opposite shows him competing as No. 55 at Kalorama (Victoria) in 1962 in a 'motorkhana' event. He certainly got stuck in, and perhaps this contributed to the fatigue cracks in the chassis that caused Max Kennedy to scrap it and replace it with No. 7258. The principal deviations from original configuration are an increase in the size of the boot, probably in the UK in the 1930s, the layout and content of the instrument panel, probably in the '60s, and the replacement of the chassis (originally No. 7278) by No. 7192, which was taken from the 'Broken Hill' car in the 1970s.

I bought my first Alvis, a TA14 saloon, from an Adelaide dealer on Boxing Day 1966, and I still have it. It was in Adelaide in the late '60s that I first encountered a front wheel drive and remember being awestruck by it. That was back in university days and subsequently work, marriage, houses, children and so on mitigated against any aspirations I might have had of owning one. Knowledge of the car's outstanding technical innovation and impressive competition record kept me intrigued and I had my eye on one magnificent example (Australia is fortunately over-represented with such machines), but I could not persuade the owner to part with it. In doing some backgrounding, I rang Bob Blacket in Sydney and learned that he was considering selling his; if that was the case, I was considering buying, and we quickly agreed on a price and I took delivery about three weeks later. I've had the car for a fortnight and, so far, my expectations have been amply fulfilled. She's well-endowed with power, rides beautifully (compared with a 12/50), handles extremely well and has a delightful gearbox. It's not surprising that they were highly competitive in their day.

Whether or not the car will return to competition I don't know. It will be the 'Zero Car' at the forthcoming Lufra Hillclimb in August 2017, but all and sundry are urging me to involve the car in the occasional historic race meeting. We'll see.

Mike Williams

With Les Lee, the owner, possibly driving, the car is seen in competition at Kalorama, Victoria, in 1962. (Mike Williams Collection)

Kalorama in the 1950s; the adjacent FWD is TV 100, nicknamed Terminal Velocity and owned by Nic Davies. (Mike Williams Collection)

A front view of the front-wheel drive at Kalorama. (Mike Williams Collection)

ALVIS CARS IN COMPETITION

Car Details: 1929 Silver Eagle TA 16.95; Registration No. BF 7869; Chassis No. 7336; Engine No. 7860; Car No. 12176; Body Maker – Replica Beetleback.

This car originally left the factory on 9 December 1929 as a Silver Eagle TA16.95 Car No. 12176. I bought the kit of parts from Jim Evans, my friend and ace engineer, in 2013.

When purchased it was decided to resurrect the car as a 1929 Silver Eagle Beetleback. Jim offered to build the car with a replica Beetleback body for me, and it would be eligible for VSCC events and historic rallies, such as The Flying Scotsman.

The engine modifications are a steel crank, flywheel, rods and high compression pistons with a compression ratio of 9:1, a modified cylinder head with oversize valves and stronger springs high lift rockers and a special camshaft. Three ¼-inch SUs and a repositioned exhaust manifold that exits through the aluminium crankcase have also been included. The results of the dyno testing were very promising, with 144 bhp showing at the flywheel.

The gearbox was rebuilt using a new close ratio gear set, which was updated using 19/30 drop gears in place of standard 17/32 gears. A 4:7:1 final drive ratio was chosen. The chassis is more or less standard, but all stripped and checked with new aluminium Hartfords, and a 12-gallon aluminium fuel tank.

Brakes are converted to hydraulic with aluminium drums. It was decided to convert the throttle pedal to the right, rather than the normal centre position, partly from a safety perspective as that is what I am used to, and partly so I don't have to think about it when trying to ascend a hill as quickly as possible. Jim constructed the ash frame. The body and wings were panelled in aluminium. Although the work took longer than expected, the important thing was to get the car right, rather than rush the job.

The car was completed in 2016 and I entered the VSCC Harewood Hillclimb, where it achieved first in class (although there were only two of us in the class), despite a sticking gear lever. Further results in VSCC hillclimbs showed second in class at the VSCC Shelsley Walsh Hillclimb.

In the next event, the car achieved a first in a very competitive class at the prestigious fully subscribed VSCC Prescott August Meeting. Two historic rallies were entered in 2016, the first of which was the 1,000 Mile Trial from Edinburgh to the RAC Headquarters in Epsom, Surrey. This is a five-day trial, running through the Scottish Borders, northern England, the Midlands and southwards towards London. However, my run resulted in a DNF when a core plug blew; although temporary repairs were made, water subsequently discharged again, this time into the magneto, with fatal results.

A better result of fifth overall was achieved in September 2016 on the Alpine Trial, held in the French Alps, starting from Divonne-les-bains, near Geneva, and finishing in Annecy, France. I am looking forward to entering more exciting competitive events with the Alvis.

Paul Wignall

Ascending a hill in the Scottish countryside during the 2016 1,000 Mile Trial Rally are Paul Wignall and Mark Appleton. (Tony Large)

Competing at Fortune Race Circuit near Edinburgh during the 2016 1,000 Mile Trial Rally; note the offside tyre deformation. (Tony Large)

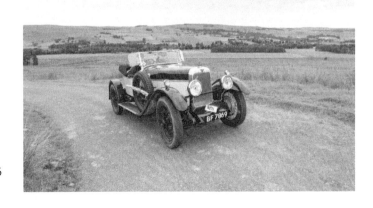

Climbing a summit during the 2016 1,000 Mile Trial. (Tony Large)

ALVIS CARS IN COMPETITION

Car Details: 1929 FD 12/75 FWD Le Mans Replica; Registration No. SC 4076; Car No. 12124.

In 1980 I wanted an interesting restoration project, and via the VSCC Newsletter, Chris Lee called about an Alvis front wheel drive. They were built between 1928 and 1929, producing only 149. It was an advanced design, intended for experienced drivers, with independent suspension and an optional supercharged engine producing 75 bhp at £625. This model won the 1½-litre class in the 1928 Le Mans 24-hour race. It was a difficult and complicated car to maintain, and was not popular with insurance companies, and Alvis stopped production in 1929.

The car was original, dismantled and complete excluding bodywork, but included a new ash frame. It had been stored for over ten years in the open, with the gearbox cover removed. Someone had engaged two gears at once and broke several gears, and the cost of replacements had exceeded the value of the car. I decided to buy the car, rebuilding the gearbox; the engine had new pistons and valves. Body panels were excellently made by Rod Jolley, and fabric covering and trim to a high standard by Wessex Car Trimming.

It went on the road in 1982 and was a joy to drive. It had excellent handling and performance from the blown engine. It sounded good as well, with the straight cut final drive and gear wheels singing in harmony! I entered some driving tests and sprints, and the 1989 VSCC Donington Race Meeting. It was great fun, and I was hooked, racing at Silverstone, Brands Hatch, Mallory Park, Croix en Ternois, Val de Vienne, Angoulême and Montlhéry in France. I also enjoyed hillclimbs at Prescott, Shelsley Walsh, Wiscombe Park plus various sprints.

In the early days it was not totally reliable; overheating caused a cracked cylinder head, which was cured by a new radiator core, and I had a crankshaft break and a final drive pinion shear. However, these were all sorted out, and it gave years of reliable and enjoyable motor sport. I sadly sold the car three years ago, as it was not getting the use it deserved. The current owner, Mark Hayward, is using it in competition with, I believe, great enjoyment.

Ian Horner

I wanted to compete in hillclimbs, sprints and races. The FWD is quirky, and I like quirky. It is loud and needs to be driven with a firm hand as the wheels want to pull you straight all the time. Ian Horner was disposing of his car, SC 4076, which he bought in 1980 as a kit of parts from where it had spent most of its life in South Wales.

Phil Scarfe bought the car in 1950 for £50 from a man in Swansea and the original Le Mans body had been chopped about since being supplied to the first owner from North Worcester Garage in Stourbridge in 1928. The Supercharger had been removed and a Stromberg carburettor installed. In 2015 I purchased the car, and competed in 2016 at Silverstone, Pembrey, Prescott and Castle Combe. I have fitted an original Solex carburettor and sorted the leaking water pump. 2017 will be a year to fix all the things that prevented the car from winning more in 2016, including new shock absorbers, available on 1929 cars, to cure the axle tramp occurring between 80 and 85 mph. Some spectators even came up to me after races to say they thought the front wheels were about to fall off. In addition to that I want to coax some more power from the 1,500cc engine in the hope of winning more. However, first standard Vintage at Pembrey and second standard Vintage at Prescott is a start.

Mark Hayward

An offside view of the car on the trailer to home. (Ian Horner)

Ian Horner at the Semi-Circle, Prescott. (Ian Horner Collection)

Mark Hayward ahead of the MG at the 2016 Castle Combe Classic. (Mike Bews)

ALVIS CARS IN COMPETITION

Car Details: 1929 TA16.95 Silver Eagle; Registration No. 4718; Chassis No. 7809; Engine No. 8265; Car No. 12665; Body Maker – Martin & King, Melbourne, Australia, later by Les Lees, Australia.

We were keen Alvis owners, competing at VSCC events and attending various Alvis outings, including interstate rallies, and the opportunity to purchase the Silver Eagle popped up. We had been overtaken at speed by Alf and Moira Wilson in this car at several events, so when the car became available we jumped at it.

We bought the car in June 2002. Alf took me for a drive in it and I was hooked. He made the gear change seem like we were driving an automatic, but then he had been driving it for approximately thirty-six years. I quickly realised that I am a long way from his prowess with the gear change; in fact, I couldn't change gear smoothly at all for a while, but I am slowly improving.

The car was originally exported to Australia as a chassis and was bodied in Melbourne by Martin & King. In the 1950s the body was replaced by then owner Les Lees to his own quirky design, which remains on the car today. Originally without a windscreen, we have added this small comfort.

Since the 1950s the car has been used in all forms of competition by a succession of owners, as well as being used as everyday transport in the 1950s through to the 1970s.

We have been involved in a variety of competition and club events, including many local and interstate tours. The car has competed successfully at Mt Tarrengower hillclimb (Central Victoria) and at the Rob Roy hillclimb. Although not fast in hillclimb terms, it is substantially faster than the Firefly that I had previously competed in and has managed to give me the occasional fright.

The Silver Eagle has also competed in a few regularity events at Phillip Island Raceway, which was a great experience. The car is reasonably quick, which is to our liking, and requires respect and a strong hand to get the best out of it.

Dale and Maritta Parsell

NSW seen in autumnal orange during the Alvis National Rally. The rally included driving around Bathurst several times, which was scary the first time, even at 60 kph. (Dale Parsell)

Competing at the Rob Roy Hillclimb in 2012. (Dale Parsell Collection)

On the return run down the hill with a friendly marshal at Morwell Hillclimb in 2011. (Dale Parsell Collection)

ALVIS CARS IN COMPETITION

Car Details: 1930 Avon Alvis; Registration No. UU 666, later Standard Avon BV 304; Avon Chassis and 1927 Alvis 12/50 Engine bored to 73 mm = 1,843 cc with a Close Ratio 12/50 Gearbox.

A friend bought my 1929 Standard Avon and sourced an original engine for it, buying a complete 1930 model for £9. I towed it back from the breakers and removed the engine and gearbox. Having no use or storage for the remaining parts he gave me everything, complete with a log book. Thus began the history of the Avon-Alvis in 1966. I was impressed with the rigidity of the chassis and that I could lift it easily. I had a 1929 SD Alvis 12/50, bought in 1957 for £20, which was my everyday car. Obviously, to me, a combination of the two would make a rapid and reliable vintage racing car, and I entered a race at Silverstone in 1971.

The bodywork was based on the single-seat design on a Maserati pictured at Brooklands. It met with approval from Lord Montague and William Boddy, who thought it 'very Brooklands', but Denis Jenkinson declared it 'abominably ugly'. Its best result was fourth place in a handicap event at Silverstone, where I started from scratch and put in the fastest lap at 62+ mph.

My career in music was being neglected so I put vintage racing aside and finally gained an MA degree in music education. However, I continued to improve my driving ability and returned to the track in the '80s with a Riley 1.5, followed by a Vauxhall Magnum previously raced by Ivan Dutton and Tony Lanfranchi. In this car I actually won a race in torrential conditions at Lydden Hill, Kent. I finished my classic saloon racing in a 1949 Morris Minor, which is still being raced today in other hands.

In order to gain more ground clearance, I shortened the sump by 2½ inches. This presented problems with oil surge on right-hand bends, necessitating a dry sump system, which I designed. A pre-selector gearbox was experimented with, but I returned to a 12/50 gearbox owing to the huge difference in weight. I later returned to competition using the pre-selector gearbox at Harewood hillclimb in 2007, but was woefully slow at 94.26 seconds.

In 2015 we returned to Silverstone with the engine properly tuned and good tyres. Although the speedometer showed 90 mph on the main straight, I was not as quick as I was forty-five years before, with a best speed of 59.6 mph. At Oulton Park I entered two races, but the water pump drive gave up on me. Hoping for a better season in 2016, I was soon to be disappointed at Silverstone, with the engine unaccountably down on power, a top speed of 80 mph and a fastest lap of 56 mph. Then, at Oulton Park the power was even lower, the car being slower in top gear than third. However, in the wet practice I was nineteenth out of thirty cars – never getting out of third gear! Descending oil pressure finally put paid to 2016. Some compensation came in the VSCC Bulletin report, which included a good picture of the Avon-Alvis and an encouraging comment from a spectator who 'liked my style'.

Alan Harpley

The Alvis 12/50 UU 666 outside the garage in Teddington, Middlesex, England. (Alan Harpley Collection)

With Brooklands-style bodywork, the car is seen on the start line at Silverstone in 1971. (Alan Harpley Collection)

Exiting the chicane at Donington. (Mark Ballard)

ALVIS CARS IN COMPETITION

Car Details: 1930 Silver Eagle TA 16.95; Registration No. KR 3147; Chassis No. 7978; Engine No. 8663; Car No. 12825; Body Maker – Darracq.

This Alvis appears on page 528 of The Vintage Alvis, written by Peter Hull and Norman Johnson, and is the most distinguished post-war Silver Eagle and the equivalent to the Green Car and the Black Car's pre-war history.

Henlys, in London, sold the car in March 1930 as a blue Cross & Ellis wide two-seater tourer with black wings and wheels, but in 1945 it was converted into a pick-up truck and was used by a greengrocer. In 1952 it was purchased by John Rowley's father's business in Walsall.

During 1954, Russell Noble (father of the current owner, Tim) bought it. Rubery Owen's mobile welding gang shortened the chassis by 12 inches and chopped the prop shaft. He fitted a home-made lightweight narrow two-seater body for £50 with a tubular steel frame and pop-riveted aluminium panels. In 1956 he won the VSCC's premier annual aggregate trophy, the Lycett, and was the only Alvis driver, except Lou Wickham in 1989, to win the trophy between 1935 and 1994. Russell also had many class wins and awards.

Stan Waine improved the car's performance in the mid-1950s by raising the compression ratio to 8.5:1, cleaning up the ports and combustion chambers and making up a four-branch exhaust manifold. The Alvis studded wheels were changed by welding Rudge hubs onto the Alvis centres and fitting 18-inch SS Jaguar multi-spoked wheels. This made it easier to fit different diameter wheels.

Around 1958, a four-seater tourer body, reputably from a 1924 12/32 Talbot Darracq, was purchased from Tony Jones for £25. The body was far too long for the Silver Eagle and the scuttle was the wrong shape. These problems were overcome by chopping out the rear doors and making a new scuttle, which was then painted a deep blue. In 1958 a spare Silver Eagle engine was purchased from the Amal Carburettor Company for £15. The engine had been on their test bed and fitted with six Amals. It had been turned electrically to test gas flow and never fired.

In 1961 the car went to C. B. Eyre and in 1967 to Keith Hill. The engine was 'well used' and the first time out broke a con-rod, at Silverstone, so the spare engine (ex-Amal Carburettors Ltd) was fitted. This engine was tuned by raising the compression ratio, removing 180 thou. (0.18 inches) off the head and block (120 and 60). The flywheel was lightened, carburettors serviced, the unique four-branch exhaust manifold retained, with Peugeot shell bearings for the big ends. The magneto was tried but ran better on coil only, and a 4.8:1 differential was fitted.

Keith Hill used it successfully in VSCC events with many successes, including the Pomeroy Trophy in 1968 (and is the only vintage Alvis to have won it to date), the 1970 Lakeland Trial, as well as many class wins and awards plus the Proxime Accessit to the Lycett Memorial Trophy in 1972.

Subsequent owners were M. A. Ross, M. J. Ridley, Keith Hill again, his cousin A. H. G. Wilson, D. N. Cameron, Jim Whyman and myself.

Tim Noble

Russell Noble pushing on into Woodcote
Corner at the June 1954 VSCC Silverstone
Meeting. (Russell Noble Collection)

Exiting Pardon Hairpin at Prescott in 1960.
(Russell Noble Collection)

Tim Noble, with John Howard as the passenger,
challenging a hill on the VSCC Herefordshire Trial in 2003.
(Roger McDonald)

ALVIS CARS IN COMPETITION

Car Details: 1930 TJ 12/50; Registration No. UP 5113; Chassis No. 8474; Engine No. 8975 (1,645cc); Car No. 13439; Body Maker – Cross & Ellis Four-Seater Tourer.

A copy of the original car records provided by Alvis Car Engineering Co. Ltd confirms the car number as 13439, with a TJ-type chassis and a 12/50 engine, No. 8975 (1,645cc), as well as gearbox No. 7178 and rear axle No. 7194 (4.77:1 ratio). The car was supplied to the police force. Leaving the force in December 1936, UP 5113 was sold by a Leeds dealer Bob Kay to G. R. Blackburn of Bedford. In 1951 it was owned by P. W. Cheese and then in 1956 by D. J. Lilley of Lilley & Skinner.

Over the next few years UP 5113 was owned by M. H. Pile, Bruce Sandeman-Craik and a Mr Walker. By 1968 the car was owned by W. Colvill and then by Mrs Astrid Bartlett. UP 5113 was then owned by A. J. Harper and Fred Multon in Kinross.

I understand the car participated in the MCC Land's End Trial of 1957 or 1958, and UP 5113 was then laid up for quite a while and partially refurbished by Colin Caborn. In 2003 I bought the car and its life of trialling started.

The original 1,645cc engine was replaced with an Alvis 4.3 engine as we needed more power to carry a large car with four occupants up a steep muddy bank. Other modifications involved replacing the wings with shorter versions and strengthening the back springs. Other tweaks have been done over the years and the car has been trialling every year since 2003.

Three years ago the 4.3 engine was replaced with a Riley 2.4, which gave me a bit more control of the power. I have of course kept the two Alvis engines in good order, together with the original wings.

We have entered many VSCC trials over the years, from Exmoor to Scotland, together with two or three other organisations, and we have won various cups along the way, but our crowning glory is winning the VSCC Kirkstyle Plate for 2015 at the VSCC Lakeland Trial.

At the moment we can't think of any more improvements to the car. Greg Wrapson has written a book called The Boys in Blue, which covers the period of the police using Alvis cars comprehensively in the 1930s.

Duncan Arthurs

Thumbs up by Tim Gresty, Alan Brown
and Mark Brierley at the top of the
2013 Drumhouse Lakeland Trial.
(Duncan Arthurs)

Duncan Arthurs driving up to the summit
of the 2015 Drumhouse Lakeland Trial.
(www.Bertram-hill.com)

'The Victors' winning the Kirkstyle
Trophy at the 2015 VSCC Lakeland
Trial. The team consist of Duncan
Arthurs, Tim Gresty, Keith Brierley and
Alan Brown. (Duncan Arthurs Collection).

ALVIS CARS IN COMPETITION

Car Details: 1930 Silver Eagle Racer; Chassis No. 7059; Engine No. 8799.

My father was not a fan of the Alvis front wheel drive (FWD) cars, believing the works should have focussed their racing efforts on the six-cylinder Silver Eagle. He and I had always dreamed of racing a Silver Eagle Special, but had vowed never to break a restorable car. Finding the parts was a formidable task, even in the 1970s. My father found some of the needed components but died long before our vision became a reality. Nonetheless, with the help of many friends, most notably Norman Roper-Marshall and Rod Jolley, the dream finally became a reality in 1988.

We used a 12/50 chassis, a crankcase from Paul Haye, Alvis Register Bulletin editor. The rear axle came from my father's spares. We decided that the car should be lowered, achieved by outrigging the front spring mounting points and using a wide-chassis front axle. This meant shortening the rear of the chassis and the rear springs so that the car would sit horizontally. We used an original 'Silent Third' box initially, but when these gears proved to be too weak, Barry Linger made stronger straight-cut gears. We stiffened the gearbox casing with a thicker, spigoted base and installed a Godfrey Marshall supercharger, chain-driven off the crankshaft, blowing at about 16 psi, and the car is methanol-fuelled.

The car has clearly demonstrated the inherent potential of the Silver Eagle. By the mid-1990s, she was competing successfully. With over 270 bhp and almost 300 foot-pounds of torque, the car's main limitations are its weight and road holding. In retrospect, it was perhaps a mistake to shorten the chassis, as I have subsequently raced Silver Eagles in sports car form and their handling is superb.

Several years elapsed before the car realized its full potential. Significant successes were achieved: second place in the Itala Trophy race; first places at Colerne Sprint at 128 mph and Curborough Sprint; setting a new class record at Loton Park Hillclimb; first at Silverstone in a five-lap handicap race; second at the Pembrey Holland Trophy race; second in the Vintage class at the Prescott Hillclimb; second overall in an eight-lap Vintage scratch race at Croix-en-Ternois; second in five-lap scratch race driven by Duncan Ricketts; and third in a pre-1936 two-seat scratch race.

In 1994 the car came of age after five years of wrestling with various development problems. She had proven herself successful in hillclimbs, sprints and races, and was more than competitive with Type 35B Bugattis, which had been our goal. Early the following year, in 1995, we found that the Alvis had won the previous year's VSCC's Alvis Trophy, had come second in the Lycett Trophy and third in the Lycett Memorial Trophy. These results were unprecedented because I had not competed in any trials or rallies but only in speed and race events.

My two proudest moments with the car came at the October 1996 Brooklands Sprint, beating Mark Gillies in the ERA-engined Brooke Special, the racer crossing the line in 14.78 seconds at 100 mph to the Brooke's 15.03 seconds at 101 mph, winning FTD! My good friend Rivers Fletcher said in his delightfully idiosyncratic style, 'Imagine that, a vintage Silver Eagle with an FTD at Brooklands!'

In 2001, the racer won the Itala Trophy race at Silverstone, beating Stanley Mann's 8-litre Bentley into second place after a tough battle. Additionally, my ERA R4D won the Patrick Lindsay Trophy race, so we had won both the VSCC's premier Vintage and Post-Vintage races at the same meeting — a feat that I was told had never been achieved before.

Mac Hulbert

Winning my first trophy – the Holland Trophy – in the Silver Eagle Racer at VSCC Pembrey, Wales, in 1995. (Terence Brettell)

Leading in the Holland Trophy Race at Cadwell Park in 2003. (Steve Welsh)

VSCC Prescott, exiting Orchard. (Bob Light)

ALVIS CARS IN COMPETITION

Car Details: 1931 12/60; Registration No. TM 9057; Chassis No. 8880; Engine No. 9435; Car No. 13718; Body Maker – Carbodies.

TM 9057 was ordered by Messrs. Dunham & Haines, Alvis dealers of Castle Street, Luton, in 1931, with the explicit instructions on the build sheet that it should be tuned for track work. Thus, its departure from normal specification featured a close ratio gearbox, a high compression head and a higher ratio back axle, there being no hills on the Brooklands race track.

The car was delivered in May 1931, and after testing and tuning was entered in several events at the historic venue. It had modest success, with a highest lap speed of 84 mph, driven by Gerald Dunham and his German lady friend Lotte (Charlotte) Schwedler. It had several third-place finishes and, encouraged by this, was later entered by Dunham in the Duke of York's Handicap in mid-1932. Watched by the Duke and Duchess of York (later King George VI and Queen Elizabeth), another third place was achieved. After 1932, it was deemed to be no longer competitive, and the Dunham team moved on to six-cylinder Alvises. TM 9057 was sold.

With the exception of a few months in 1948, we have the entire history of the car. It changed hands several times, and was eventually purchased by Londoner Francis Spencer from a garage near Truro. It was later driven by Spencer in many VSCC speed, sprint and trial events. It has raced at Brands Hatch, Castle Combe, Llandow, Thruxton, Silverstone and Oulton Park, and taken part in sprint and hillclimb events at Gaydon, Prescott and Wiscombe Park. It raced at the last event held at the old Crystal Palace circuit, where it finished fourth. It has also been demonstrated at both Le Mans and the Isle of Man TT course. Spencer had the car for about fifty years, and only sold it because of failing eyesight.

TM 9057 was invited back to Brooklands for an event in 2007 and another in 2011. Articles in Motorsport, the VSCC archives, William Boddy's History of Brooklands and my own research confirm its Brooklands history.

I have owned the car for the past six or seven years, and steadily improved its rather tired condition. It has had a comprehensive engine rebuild, complete with a new Phoenix crank and rods, new pistons and timing gears, followed by a re-trim, paint and a new hood. It now runs very well, and has been used on numerous long-distance rallies.

Alan Cook

Gerry Dunham preparing
to race in the paddock at
Brooklands on 4 July 1931.
(Richard Dunham)

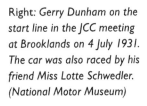

Right: *Gerry Dunham on the
start line in the JCC meeting
at Brooklands on 4 July 1931.
The car was also raced by his
friend Miss Lotte Schwedler.*
(National Motor Museum)

Below: *Francis Spencer racing
at VSCC Silverstone on 31 July
1965.* (Harold Barker)

ALVIS CARS IN COMPETITION

Car Details: 1931 TK 12/60 Two-Seater Sports; Registration No. GO 2619; Chassis No. 8766; Engine No. 9358; Car No. 13628; Body Maker – Carbodies.

In 1968 I was already a keen Alvis owner, driving a Firefly as an everyday car. I had heard that there was a 12/60 stored in a local village only a few miles away from where I lived. I tracked it down and did manage to see the car but the owner was abroad and it took several months before I finally got the call to say that the car was for sale.

It was in a very sorry state and although I did manage to drive the car home it was clear that a full mechanical and bodywork restoration was required. This is another story but it is sufficient to say that this took many years to achieve – a common theme I am sure, but well worth the effort!

During the period that the car was off the road I began to piece together bits of its history. The original owner was a Mrs A. H. Johns from Bishop's Stortford, and after one other owner it was purchased by Alvis enthusiast Rivers Fletcher, and it was in his ownership that GO 2619 was featured in The Autocar magazine in February 1946 in the series called 'Talking of Sports Cars' No. 282.

In the Autocar article, Rivers Fletcher describes the work that he had done to the car as it had clearly suffered badly during the wartime period. When it was finished he used it for his daily transport, but also for competition events, including sprints and circuit events, as shown in his own photographs opposite. After the Second World War, Rivers Fletcher was involved in the organisation of motor sport events at Cockfosters and elsewhere.

So far I have owned GO 2619 for forty-eight years, and have obviously covered many miles; however, it is now regularly driven by both my son and I, so we have to share our driving time. Last year a small group of Alvis enthusiasts left the Midlands for a trip to Shetland, Orkney and the North and West of Scotland; a trip of just over 2,000 miles, which GO 2619 completed with the minimum of fuss and maximum reliability.

When asked why I own an Alvis I think the best answer I can give is that it's because of the straightforward design and quality engineering, and this is just as relevant today as it was in 1931, when the car was new; thereby, the owner can enjoy the best of vintage motoring with maximum usability.

David Webster

Rivers Fletcher taking part in the 750 Car Club Driving Tests in 1945. (David Webster Collection)

Rivers Fletcher prepares to sprint the 12/60. Note the corduroy helmet made by Lewis & Son, London. (David Webster Collection)

Trials event in 1950. (Ex-Alvis Register Photograph Album – David Webster Collection)

ALVIS CARS IN COMPETITION

Car Details: 1931 Silver Eagle Tourer TC 16.95; Registration No. OF 9257; Engine No. 9145; Car No. 13746; Body Maker – Rod Jolley, Carbodies design.

In 1978 I took my Alvis 12/70 Special to Southwest Alvis Day, held at Sherborne House. While there, someone told me that Peter Osmond had an Alvis Silver Eagle that he was selling for spares. After Peter and I agreed on a price, I picked up my rusty prize a few weeks later. It was a sad story. The car had been used as a farm tractor until a cylinder collapsed. It was then stored in an open-fronted shed, resulting in severe rusting of the front of the chassis. Someone had sacrilegiously sawn the chassis in half to show at Bristol Classic Car Show as part of a 'before and after' exhibit. It had been tack-welded back together, and it was in a bad state.

I decided that, if possible, I should try to save the car. The late Bill Grist, another Silver Eagle devotee, had a body business, and after sandblasting the chassis he decided it was well worth saving. Bill plated the front dumb irons and applied a good rustproof paint: we had a start on a restoration.

My lifetime friend Norman Roper-Marshall volunteered to get the chassis into good shape. We used the road springs (rusty but otherwise serviceable), but bushes, brakes and brake cables, kingpins, shock absorbers and many other miscellaneous parts needed renewing. The gearbox was fitted with new constant mesh gears, transforming the spacing of the ratios to approximate those of the Silver Crest, the finest of all Alvis gearboxes.

In the late 1960s, Tony Bianchi had built a delectable Silver Eagle Alvis Special, beautifully finished, with a Brooklands-type cowl gracing a narrow two-seater body. Tony had decided to fit a Speed 25 engine to the Special, putting the original Silver Eagle engine up for sale. When I paid £350 for it my friends were horrified, but I thought I had a good buy and this lovely competition engine now solved the problem of motive power for the chassis.

The final step was to take the restored chassis to my good friend Rod Jolley. We agreed on a basic body style, and Rod produced a lovely tourer body based on a Carbodies original, as well as making a very effective full-flow exhaust system. Finished in the summer of 1984, it was the very last body that Rod produced at his home workshop before opening his premises in Lymington.

Since 1984 the car has toured Scotland, France and Eastern Europe, as well as achieving some competitive success. It won the Alvis Register Jubilee race at Donington in 1998, and has also competed at Mallory, Silverstone, Curborough, Prescott, Colerne, Whitfield Park, Cornbury Park and Loton Park with some success. Its acceleration matches that of a new Speed 25, and in it set a VSCC Loton Park record for vintage standard and modified cars in the 1,501–3,000cc class, which stood for some years until Chris Podger in the Green Car, GO 5151, beat it.

Mac Hulbert

Competing in the VSCC Jubilee Sprint Meeting at Whitfield Park in 1999. (Paul Foggitt)

Resting at home, ready for more action. (Clive Taylor)

ALVIS CARS IN COMPETITION

Car Details: 1931 TJ 12/50; Registration No. NV 438; Chassis No. 8495; Engine No. 9478; Car No. 13855; Body Maker – Two-Seater Special.

I acquired NV 438 in the August of 1978. I was looking for a reasonably priced car to make into a VSCC Special and the 12/50 Alvis seemed ideal. One attraction was that NV 438 was already a Special, albeit a very simple one. The body was a quite nicely built tub, and the chassis had been shortened by about 9 inches. The mechanics were otherwise standard but from various models. It was a good starting point, as I did not have to cut up an otherwise good car.

I entered it for the Prescott Hillclimb and a handicap race at Silverstone, and realised how slow it was. Something had to be done. The engine was rebuilt with increased compression using Renault pistons and shaving a bit off both block and head. The camshaft was re-profiled by Blydenstein to increase overlap, and the clutch cover was replaced with an aluminium one to lighten the flywheel assembly. The single updraft Solex carburettor was replaced by two sidedraft 1¼-inch SUs and the exhaust manifold was fabricated as a fairly efficient outside system. A rev. counter drive was belt driven from the nose of the crankshaft, and the whole assembly was dynamically balanced.

The chassis was not ignored, the brakes were overhauled and relined (the 12/50 brakes are quite effective if in good order), the kingpins and steering joints were replaced, as were the shackle pins and bushes. The springs had already been flattened when the chassis was shortened, so all that was needed here was to fit heavier Hartford dampers. The car went and handled very much better after this treatment, so I entered it for VSCC handicap races at Silverstone, Cadwell Park and Castle Combe. The best result was a third at Cadwell, but it was all good fun, and I was now able to beat my rival in Persil 2!

I also entered various vintage hillclimbs, at Prescott, Shelsley Walsh, Loton Park and Wiscombe Park. Sprint meetings were entered at Colerne, Brooklands, Weston-super-Mare and Goodwood. The standard gear ratios were not really suitable for these, so a close ratio gear set was then fitted. At about this time I thought that something ought to be done about the appearance of the car. The pointed tail was constructed, and a much more elegant set of wings fitted. The car was then repainted in the same shade of blue, but to a much higher standard.

The car was used quite extensively on the road, being driven to local meetings as well as competitive events, and a vee-windscreen had been fitted for road use. It handled very nicely on the road, with quite a good turn of speed and very precise steering. It was at its best on good country main roads. Sometime later it was entered for a VSCC vintage Alvis race at Donington with Jane Tomlinson, the present owner, driving. She performed very creditably, and bought the car from me in June 2014. Jane intends to continue to use it in VSCC sprints and hillclimbs. Past events are listed below:

VSCC Races: Silverstone; Cadwell Park; Castle Combe; Donington.
VSCC Sprints: Colerne, best time 38 seconds; Brooklands, best time 60.4 seconds; Goodwood, best time 1 minute 4.7 seconds; Weston-super-Mare.
VSCC Hillclimbs: Prescott, best time 55.4 seconds; Loton Park, best time 83.9 seconds; Wiscombe Park, best time 63.01 seconds; Shelsley Walsh, best time 52.07 seconds.

Nigel Walder

In original form at Silverstone in 1983. (Nigel Walder Collection)

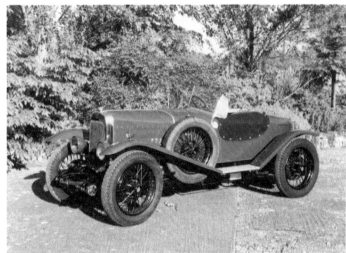

The nearside view of the car in revised form in 1995. (Nigel Walder)

On the start line at Shelsley Walsh in 1993. (Nigel Walder Collection)

POST-VINTAGE PERIOD: 1932 TO 1940

Car Details: 1932 Speed 20 SA; Registration No. L J 6969; Chassis No. 15023; Engine No.10553; Body Maker – Cross & Ellis.

I acquired my Alvis Speed 20 SA with 4.3 engine and Silver Crest gearbox from Rod Jolley around 1999, and it took me more than a year to convince him and his lovely family to sell the car to me. It is a magnificent car and provides immense enjoyment. This Alvis can go anywhere and has been entered in and finished several long-distance rallies.

These include two Peking to Paris rallies in 2007 and 2010, where the car finished in both events in fourth place overall. European Rallies also have been entered, such as the Scottish Malts, Liège–Rome–Liège, several Rallye des Alpes and the Ardennes Bleue.

The car has been taken to South Africa to enter three Classic Safari rallies: Capetown SA–Namibia–Botswana–Zimbabwe, South Africa–Capetown–Mombasa–Dar-es-Salam/Tanzania–Malawi–Mozambique, South Africa–Lesotho–Capetown, where the car was the overall winner.

Other adventures in the Alvis were to enter the London to Casablanca Rally, and the Road to Mandalay Rally, starting from Singapore through Malaysia, Thailand and Myanmar. Later on we travelled to Australia, starting from Melbourne via Adelaide, Coober Pedy and Alice Springs, and westwards to Uluru, the Tanami Track, the Kimberley, Kakadu and Darwin.

Due to her reliability and 'torquey' engine she has always finished on the podium, or has at least been a class winner.

The car has been raced successfully at Donington, Silverstone, Zandvoort, Portimao, and Nürburgring Nordschleife! At the Nürburgring Nordschleife in 2005 the car was entered in a long-distance 500 km race, finishing in the mid-field. This was the first and last time in history that a pre-war car had competed in a long-distance 500 km race on the Nordschleife, as all other entries were racing cars from the 1950s to '80s.

Competing in the 2005 Tour of Britannia, the car was overall winner on index of performance that included races at Cadwell Park, Rockingham and Silverstone. As a result of this performance, the organizers awarded the prestigious Johnny Wakefield Trophy, which since 1951 has been presented every year to the racing driver with the fastest lap of the season at Silverstone. The trophy lives in the BRDC clubhouse, Silverstone, England.

So far I have certainly travelled more than 100,000 miles in this car on long-distance rallies and racing events wherever possible, and it has been an exhilarating and unique experience.

Rüdi Friedrichs

The September 2011 Classic Safari Rally on day 16 at Cathedral Park, near Lesotho/Maseru, South Africa. (Gerard Brown)

The September 2011 Classic Safari Rally on day 16 at Driekloof Dam, which is part of the Sterkfontein Dam, Free State, South Africa. (Rüdi Friedrichs)

The 2012 Australian Rally at Uluru/ Ayers Rock on the Lassetter Highway in the Southern area of the Northern Territory. (Rüdi Friedrichs)

ALVIS CARS IN COMPETITION

Car Details: 1932 TJ 12/50; Registration No. DG 3666; Chassis No. 9278; Engine No. 9425; Body Maker – Cross & Ellis.

While we were touring the Cotswolds in 1970, my wife Sue and I were told about an open Alvis lying at the back of a garage in a nearby town. On the way home we located the garage and sure enough, right at the back, covered in tyres, boxes and sundry rubbish, was DG 3666, a 1932 TJ 12/50 four-seater tourer. An examination proved the car to be complete and sound so a deal was struck. The following week I returned with a trailer and rescued DG.

Once back at our cottage in Outwoods, Shropshire, I started on a fairly comprehensive overhaul, including to the engine, wiring, kingpins, floorboards and weather equipment. Taxed, with an MOT and back on the road, DG proved to be a superb touring car with light steering, excellent road holding and an easy 55 to 60 mph cruising speed.

Experience of competing previously with ND 2345, my 1923 12/40 Alvis tourer had given me a taste for motorsport and DG was duly entered in various events, although I decided not to do circuit racing but to stick to sprints, hillclimbs and rallies.

DG was successful at Curborough Sprint, where I knew the course well, and also at Gaydon, where the fast-open course with various chicanes really suited DG's superb handling. 1972 was a particularly good season and DG won the Alvis Owner Club Midland Trophy, as well as the Martin Smith Trophy.

In spite of my love for the early sub-frame 12/50s, I really rated the TJ chassis, which has better handling, brakes and lighter steering. After my initial fettling, DG only ever required routine servicing and I covered a considerable mileage touring within the UK, and attending VSCC and AOC events.

I sold DG in about 1973 and subsequently reacquired her in the '90s before part-exchanging DG for a Silver Eagle tourer – a big mistake. DG then passed to Dr Charles Moon, who still has this very fine Alvis.

Mike Ridley

Our TJ 12/50 tourer, DG.
(Mike Ridley)

The offside rear view of the
Cross & Ellis body. (Mike Ridley)

The offside front view of the
Cross & Ellis body. (Mike Ridley)

ALVIS CARS IN COMPETITION

Car Details: 1932 Firefly Special; Registration No. 131 GMO; Chassis No. 9994; Engine; Crested Eagle TF; Body Maker – Special.

John Carpenter built the car in the early 1960s using a 1932 Firefly chassis, No. 9994. John was ex-Royal Air Force, then a civil pilot with Jersey Airlines. He found the chassis in Jersey without bodywork. The open tourer body built by John is styled on a 3-litre Bentley and very lightweight, using an ash frame, clad in marine ply and covered in leather cloth, and is very strong. John was very competitive in sprints and eventually broke the crankshaft on the Firefly engine in 1969, replacing it with the same type. This crankshaft also broke in 1973 and the engine was replaced with a Speed 20 unit in 1977.

   John had great success with this engine at Brooklands Meetings in the '80s, enjoying racing pairs on part of the banked circuit. John maintained a detail log not only of the build of the car, but also of the competition results:

Brooklands, June 1983: *Byfleet Pairs Sprint. Beat L-type Magna.*
Brooklands AOC Meeting Hillclimb Result, October 1983: *Firefly Special 12.13 seconds. Rivers Fletcher 4.3-litre 10.59 seconds. Winner PVT. White Racing Alvis 12/50 10.59 seconds. Winner vintage 12/70 light Special 11 seconds. Runner-up PVT.*
Brooklands, June 1985: *Three sprints along banking. Went like a train – no opposition. Lags afraid to come with me.*
Brooklands Reunion, June 1986: *Five banking runs: First – Against Tim Birkin's 4.5-litre blown Bentley single-seater. He won. Second – I beat him. Third – Riley Special. Beat him. Fourth – Against M45 Lagonda. Beat him. Fifth – Against a 4-litre Railton 8-cyl. He won.*
Brooklands Test Hillclimb Bean/Riley Meeting, July 1986: *Firefly Special time 12.0 seconds, Rivers Fletcher 10.59 seconds, Alvis 12/70 Special 11 seconds.*
Brooklands, June 1987: *All is well. No misfiring. One banking run – opposition easily vanquished. Two runway timed sprints. Both opponents beaten (Aston and Hyper Leaf). Times: 21.5 and 20 seconds.*

Just prior to passing away, John sold the car to fellow AOC member Jim Musty, who owned it for around ten years. Jim entered it in several Brooklands 'Members Meetings'. During a driving test in 2010, serious noises came from the engine. A spare Crested Eagle TF engine was installed, which had been completely rebuilt with new conrods and a lightened flywheel and now gives in excess of 90 bhp.

   The car came into my ownership just prior to Jim passing away in 2014, with the new engine nicely run in. During my ownership I have refurbished the car mechanically and renewed the electrics, but have only made subtle changes to the appearance. These days the car is used for touring and has an impressive performance.

John Worrell

Aerial front view of 131 GMO.
(John Worrell)

The offside profile. (John Worrell)

The front view. (John Worrell)

ALVIS CARS IN COMPETITION

Car Details: 1932 Speed 20 SA Tourer; Registration No. XJ 1031; Chassis No. SA9820; Engine No. 10269; Body Maker – Cross & Ellis.

I am a recent owner of this car, having acquired it in April 2015 from Michael Shelley in Essex, who had owned it since 1974. Mr Shelley had a record of all previous owners back to June 1932 and it is a 'matching numbers' car.

He had, over the years, done much restoration work, which I continued, mainly with the assistance of Earley Engineering, to get it into its present condition. The P100 lamps are not original but they have been on the car for a very long time, probably over sixty years, so I consider them a part of the history of the car and I don't intend on reverting to the original 80s, which are inferior anyway.

I was in my sixty-eighth year when I bought the car and had not had a classic car for a very long time. However, I was lucky enough to have been brought up with interesting cars and in my youth had owned a 1938 MG, a Bristol 406 and an Alvis TD 21 DHC with the ZF gearbox. I always considered the Alvis Speed models to be among the finest cars of the 1930s, so when the opportunity arose to acquire one, I went for it.

An additional deciding factor is that I have two grandsons, aged ten and twelve, and I want to foster their interest in pre-war motoring and hopefully encourage them to do a bit of gentle rallying when they are old enough to drive. To a ten-year-old, 1932 means very little, but when you say the Alvis is four years older than the first Spitfire, it brings it all into context.

The car has little past competition history and the recent photograph of it in the 2016 VSCC Welsh Rally is probably its first event for a very many years. I hope that is about to change as I pass the car down to the next generation.

Recent improvements to the car include replacing the old (but not the original) dashboard and rewiring the instruments, as well as incorporating a new fuel gauge where there had been a (non-original) clock. Previously, there had been a dipstick in the boot in lieu of the long-defunct Hobson gauge. I also had a new 14-inch electric fan fitted, but this has an 11-amp rating and the original three-brush dynamo only produced 8 amps on a good day.

I took the decision to fit a dynator (an alternator inside a replica of the original dynamo casing). Alas, to my dismay, this has invalidated my VSCC Buff Form, so that will limit my eligibility for a number of rally events. However, I feel it was the right decision as the car's electrics are now extremely reliable and the cooling system works perfectly. I have undertaken a number of long journeys in it and plan on making many more.

Hugh Sterling

The 2016 VSCC Welsh Regularity Trial. (Peter McFadyen)

In Presteigne High Street during the 2016 VSCC Welsh Regularity Trial. (Hugh Sterling)

Never mind the salt on the roads, winter motoring in freezing temperatures is exhilarating! (Hugh Sterling)

ALVIS CARS IN COMPETITION

Car Details: Giron Alvis 1932/37.

The initial seed was sown, amidst a beery haze, while sitting with my old mate Paul Holdsworth in the grandstands at a VSCC race meeting in the mid-1970s. Paul and I jotted down, on the back of a fag packet, a list of the various Alvis spares we possessed between us. We had an SA Speed 20 chassis, a Speed 25 engine, a huge Wade supercharger and an equally huge pre-selector gearbox.

We decided we would like to try to build the ultimate Alvis Special. We both possessed enthusiasm in abundance, but little in the way of race car engineering experience. Thankfully, through my connections with the National Motor Museum in Beaulieu, I had got to know and became great friends with Louis Giron, who was then a technical consultant to the museum.

Louis Giron (not to be confused with Louis Chiron) was a technical wizard, particularly famous for his work with racing Bugattis and Alfa Romeos. He was also well known as a 'press on' driver of these cars. Louis, when asked, readily agreed to help with the technical specification of the car; in fact, in the event he did an awful lot more, helping me to build the engine and introducing me to all the right people, including Gordon Allen, whose company, Allen Crankshafts, made the crank and connecting rods. I also met Amherst Villiers, of supercharger fame, through Louis, and thus gained much invaluable information and advice.

I laid out the engine and gearbox in the chassis. We decided we wanted a properly cast aluminium blower drive housing with the chain drive running in oil. I made the patterns and had the housing cast and Louis had it machined, then I was able to lay out the supercharger and devise mountings and manifolds. The next job was to draw up the body, which was loosely styled on the Mercedes Silver Arrow crossed with an Alfa Romeo 159.

With Louis's help, the engine was assembled with the new crank and rods, new forged pistons from Cosworth c/o Paul Holdsworth's old mate Keith Duckworth, which gave a static compression ratio of 8.5:1, and which Louis calculated to be around 14.5:1 at 18 lbs of boost. Needless to say, we were planning to run on methanol fuel! With the engine, transmission and supercharger installed in the chassis, I was then able to build a simple buck and make the body.

The finished car appeared at a VSCC Silverstone meeting for the first time in the late '70s. Unfortunately, it took me a further four to five years to fully understand the enormous fuel flow necessary to keep the engine happy; at 1.5 miles to a gallon, it was almost impossible to flow enough fuel through the carburettor needle valves. The constant backfires into the inlet manifold, due to weak mixture, destroyed quite a few superchargers before I realised what was causing it. Once I had sorted that out, it ran very reliably for many years.

I am not good at recording results, but I remember winning Weston-super-Mare speed trials with FTD, winning several VSCC races, and even winning races in Sweden and Spa, as well as breaking the pre-war record at Gurston Down. Probably the best result was in the Merlin Classic Meeting held on the Isle of Man in 1989, where the old car beat everything, including full race Cobras and D-type Jaguars; everything except the famous ERA R4D, and we were only just behind that. As a consequence of this performance, the organisers awarded me the 'Man of the Meeting' Award at the Villa Marina presentation in Douglas.

Rod Jolley

Louis Giron in his workshop. He was co-designer of the car, with Paul Holdsworth and Rod Jolley. (National Motor Museum)

Paul Holdsworth with Rod Jolley in the car at VSCC Oulton Park. (Clive Taylor)

Flat out at 135 mph on 18-inch wheels with wheel spin at Montlhéry, France! (Rod Jolley Collection)

ALVIS CARS IN COMPETITION

Car Details: 1932 Firefly/4.3; Registration No. 998 UYF; Chassis No. 9981; Engine No. 13551; Body Maker – Special.

After almost two decades of successful and extraordinary joyful rallying and also racing my Speed 20 SA, my friend Wolfgang and I wanted to restore and set up a proper Alvis for racing only.

It was my good friend Rod Jolley who provided us with Firefly chassis No. 9981 and engine No. 13551, modified to 4.3-litre specifications – an ideal combination for setting up a competitive race Alvis in early 2013.

The restoration took nearly two years of attention to every detail, maintaining the heritage and setting up the technology to original specifications, and using only original Alvis components. The result was a very competitive, light Firefly chassis fitted with a very strong and torquey 4.3 Alvis engine and a strong and reliable Alvis Silvercrest gearbox.

The project was successfully finished early 2014 and we rolled out the car for the first time in the Motor Racing Legends Pre-War Race in Portimao, finishing second overall, beating even a Bugatti 35B.

The performance and reliability of the car and the engine was amazing – we have revved the engine up to 5,000 revs without any problems, and the only car we have never been able to beat was the Frazer Nash Supersports of Fred Wakeman and Patrick Blakeney-Edwards.

The following year, in May 2015, we raced the car at Donington in the 'Mad Jack' for Pre-War Sportscars and again came second overall, only being beaten by the Frazer Nash.

In July 2015 we entered the Silverstone Classics, Kidston Trophy for Pre-War Sportscars and finished third overall, and in October, in Portimao again, we finished second overall.

April 2016 saw the car at Silverstone again for the VSCC Spring Start. It won the Silverstone Trophy overall, which was certainly the biggest success so far. In May 2016 we were second overall again at Donington and fourth overall at Zandvoort, Holland, due to a lost bolt on the float chamber–carburettor connection.

This is the short but pretty successful race history of this Alvis Firefly so far, which will certainly be continued into the long-term future. It is a good proof of what great technology Alvis had developed in the early 1930s.

Rüdi Friedrichs

Exiting and climbing up a hill in Europe. (Rüdi Friedrichs Collection)

Accelerating away from the pack. (Rüdi Friedrichs Collection)

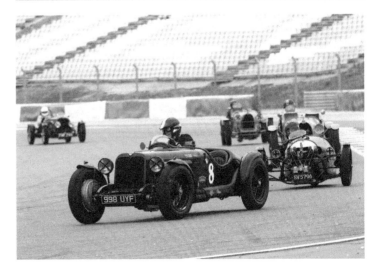

Leading the bunch, ahead of the Morgan and Bugattis. (Rüdi Friedrichs Collection)

ALVIS CARS IN COMPETITION

Car Details: 1932 Speed 20 SA; Registration No. YY 2583; Chassis No. 9888; Engine No. 10388; Body Maker – Replica VdP.

In 1932 the chassis only (No. 9888) was dispatched to Charles Follett, to have a Vanden Plas body fitted (No. 1813). The first registered owner was David Robertson in Chew Magna, Somerset. Between 1957 and 1959 the car spent some time at Cranwell in the ownership of three consecutive RAF officers. Later on, the car fell onto hard times after the body had been removed and the chassis languished somewhere in Wales for a long time. It was discovered in 1992 and brought to London. Nic Simpson was approached to sell it and he did so to Carel de Bruin.

There is a comprehensive article written by Carel, published in the Alvis Owner Bulletin No. 470 in 2001, covering the discovery and restoration process by Nic Simpson and completed by Carel de Bruin in Holland. During Carel's ownership, the car was awarded the Herbert Trophy for the Best Speed 20 at the 75th Alvis Anniversary in 1998, held at Brooklands – a great achievement and honour.

During 2013 Nic was instructed to sell the car and I became the next owner. My wife and I have done around fifty classic car rallies all over the world, ranging from serious endurance events lasting over a month and covering 10,000 miles (such as two Peking to Paris, London–Sydney, two South America, three Classic Safaris, etc.) to typical weekend rallies, all of them driving classics from the '50s and '60s.

The Speed 20 is our first (and so far, only) pre-war car, and we were naturally curious (and at the same time slightly worried) of how we would adapt to the differences – the central throttle, crash gearbox and so on. However, it was a very pleasant surprise. It is roomy, the engine is reasonably powerful and the chassis is responsive and neutral. The brakes are quite acceptable (cables are adjustable from the driver's position) and the steering is precise and not very heavy (although the turning radius is too large).

The car is mechanically standard with no major add-ons. We fitted an electric fan on the radiator, because we will eventually drive it down to Portugal, and an electric fuel pump to add to fill up the carburettors at the start. We tried a slightly longer differential ratio (because of the need for some motorway or long-distance driving) but decided to go back to the original. We missed the torque...

We have competed in four rallies in the Speed 20: two Flying Scotsman rallies and two 1,000 Mile Trials, each at around 1,000 miles in length. We won third place in our class in the 2016 Flying Scotsman and the Concours d'Elegance prize on the 2016 1,000 Mile Trial. This was a special achievement, especially for a car with a replica body and in the face of very strong competition.

We finished those four rallies with no major breakdowns and no punctures. The only unpleasant occurrence was when we broke both windscreen mounts and had to endure heavy rain on our faces. Up to now we have only entered short rallies in the UK; three to six days, close to home and spare parts in case something goes wrong, and only open to pre-war cars. My wife Maria feels so comfortable and secure in the Alvis that she insisted we take her to Japan in April 2017 for the Samurai Challenge, a three-week and 3,500-mile-long rally.

This would be our first really long event in it, longer and very far away, an event we could have entered in any one of our tried and trusted post-war classics.

Since writing this story prior to April, I am pleased to say that we completed the Samurai Rally without any incidents, which I think says a lot about how we feel about the Alvis Speed 20 SA tourer.

Jose Romoa de Sousa

The 2014 HERO 1,000 Mile Trial – Jose and Maria taking a left turn in the country. (Photograph © Blue Passion)

The 2014 HERO 1,000 Mile Trial – Jose and Maria driving through the ford. (Tony Large)

The 2017 Samurai Rally in Japan, with Mount Fuji in the background. (Jose Romao de Sousa Collection)

ALVIS CARS IN COMPETITION

Car Details: 1932 Speed 20 SA; Registration No. JSJ 742, previously OJ 3; Chassis No. 10008; Engine No. 10457; Car No. 14678; Body Maker – Charlesworth Sports Saloon (Special Body).

This car was commissioned as a motor car for rallying and is therefore unique. Purchase price when new, including accessories, was £910 18s 6d. The original colour of the car was black with green upholstery and carpets, with grey watered silk head cushions with black silk piping. The straight-six OHV engine gave 2,511cc, offering 19.82 hp, with a maximum speed of 95 mph. There are several special features such as scalloped running boards, phosphor bronze cylinder head, all round cable brakes, Carl Zeiss flexible combined lamps and wing mirrors, a panoramic convex rear-view mirror to cover the view of the rear side quarters and a vertically split driver's door window.

The front section winds up and down as any conventional window, with the mechanism only in the front of the door. The rear section window is fixed, which enabled a recess to be installed beneath in the door to allow for the introduction of an arm rest for the driver, as there is no mechanism in the way. Mr Alan W. F. Smith of Stepney Laundry, London, the original owner, even instructed that the windscreen wiper motor was to be installed at the bottom of the windscreen, so that his vision through the windscreen was not impaired in any way.

Mr Smith part-exchange traded an MG and Humber against the Alvis. The Humber registration was GO 4, which he hoped to transfer to the Alvis; however, the Birmingham authorities would not allow this. Mr Smith intended to enter OJ 3 in the Monte Carlo Rally, but the modifications he had requested from the Alvis Motor Company and Charlesworth had not been completed in time, and to quote Mr Smith's letter of January 1933 to Charlesworth, 'In its present condition the car would not [have stood] a very good chance.'

OJ 3 was entered in the 1933 RAC Rally, finishing twenty-fourth out of ninety-four. The following year it was entered again and finished in eighteenth place out of eighty-eight. The family used OJ 3 until 1948, after which it was left in a barn until 1968. When Smith died in 1968, his collection totalling 100 vehicles was sold at auction by Sotheby's. Lot No. 70, OJ 3, was sold for £320 to Mr C. Wilson. By this time, the car had travelled 28,000 miles. The car was dilapidated, but original and complete. Mr Wilson and a friend privately restored the car over four years, stripping it down to the chassis and re-building it before passing it to his son.

Mr J. Fortune, the next owner, bought the car at auction in December 1997, by which point the car had travelled 34,200 miles. During 1997 to 1999, an extensive mechanical and electrical renovation, including a complete engine re-build, took place. Professor Peter Burbridge, the next owner, acquired it on 20 September 2001, when the car had travelled about 34,850 miles.

On 14 September 2011, the current owner, Hugh Bradnum, purchased it, and has subsequently had it regularly maintained and serviced by Earley Engineering Ltd, Kingstone, Herefordshire. I am pleased to say that in 2012, at the thirty-third Bristol Classic Car Show, OJ 3 won the Best Pre-War Car Award, and featured on the Alvis stand at the 2014 NEC Classic Car Show in Birmingham.

Hugh Bradnum

Offside and frontal view. (Hugh Bradnum)

Offside rear view. (Hugh Bradnum)

Aerial display of Concours cars at the 2014 NEC Classic Car Show, Birmingham, England. (Hugh Bradnum)

ALVIS CARS IN COMPETITION

Car Details: 1933 Speed 20 SB; Registration No. BOL 229; Chassis No. 10876; Car No. 15857; Body Maker – Cross & Ellis Four-Door Tourer Body No. 30268.

This car is the sixth SB Speed 20 to be built, and was delivered to the Alvis agent Galt's in Glasgow on 30 November 1933. The car has independent front suspension and an all-synchromesh gearbox – the first production car in the world to have synchromesh on all four gears.

This Cross & Ellis tourer body featured long flowing wings, full-width running boards and concave bodywork at the rear, waisted in from the front wings. The hood folds down into a well, maintaining the long, low, slender lines, and the early SB Speed 20s have the lighter sprung front bumper.

The first private owner was twenty-one-year-old Ray Thompson, a member of a wealthy family in Cobham, Surrey, quite close to Brooklands. The car was serviced by Thompson & Taylor, who had a workshop housed in the Campbell Shed in the 'Flying Village' within the Brooklands circuit.

This firm built a number of famous cars including the 1931 and 1933 Bluebirds for Malcolm Campbell and also the Napier-Railton, which is now on display in the Brooklands Clubhouse.

Ray was keen on motor sport and paid 10s to lap Brooklands in 1936 at 78 mph in BOL 229. He entered the Speed 20 in the 1938 MCC Land's End Trial. Press photographs taken at the time show the car competing in this challenging competition. Ray entered BOL 229 in other competitive events, but specific details have been lost in the midst of time.

In 1969, when I was twenty-two years old, and having researched them and realising what spectacular cars they were, I bought the car from Ken Frith, at that time a doyen of the Alvis Owner Club and the Bentley Drivers Club. He was a pianist for the Northern Dance Orchestra and also the landlord of the Dandy Cock Inn, in Disley. He kept BOL 229 together with a variety of other pre-war Alvis and Bentley cars.

When I bought the car, it was a rather tired thirty-six-year-old, but it was all there and, most importantly, had all its original bodywork. I have gone right through the car, rebuilding every mechanical component. The bodywork was tackled in 2013. The 'B' posts and paintwork needed attention, plus there were limited woodwork repairs required, after which the car was painted all-over black (as it had been when it left the factory) together with red leather upholstery.

In 2015 the car won the Alvis Owner Club Concours Award for the best pre-war car and also the prize for the Best Car in Show at the 2015 Alvis Owner Club International Alvis Day.

David Walters

Eric Thompson driving in the MCC Land's End Trial at Crackington on 6 April 1938. (David Walters Collection)

A nearside view of the Cross & Ellis tourer body. (David Walters)

Dashboard design and folding screen erected; note the 'Brooklands' aero screens as well. (David Walters)

ALVIS CARS IN COMPETITION

Car Details: 1933 SA Speed 20 Tourer; Registration No. GOB 260; Chassis No. 10147; Engine No. 14932; Body Maker – Vanden Plas.

In July 1987 the late Mike Cummins showed me some amazing photographs of an SA Speed 20 tourer that had been walled up since 1969. The previous owner, a Mr Sprague, had owned the Alvis since the 1940s and had trolley-jacked the car into a narrow garage at his home in Kington, Herefordshire, in 1969. He then built a sectional wall to replace the garage doors, with the only access then being a single door at one end.

The car was for sale and I made an appointment for my late wife Sue and myself to see the car. The late owner's wife showed us to a rickety building at the top of the garden and when I entered my torch picked out the unmistakeable shape of a Vanden Plas Speed 20 tourer, registration number GOB 260.

The car, although very dusty, was remarkably sound, and a deal was struck over a cup of tea in the garden. A fortnight later my friend and fellow Alvis owner Rob Jones, and his son Richard, helped me to exhume GOB.

First, we dismantled the wooden wall, and then with the aid of two trolley jacks, and accompanied by much bending and creaking of floorboards, GOB was out in the open for the first time in eighteen years.

Over the next two years GOB underwent a total rebuild. As the original SA engine had been replaced by an SB unit, I decided to fit a Speed 25 engine and 3.8 differential to give GOB a real turn of speed.

After careful running in, including a trip back to Kington and the Sprague family, Sue and I entered GOB in the 1989 Paris–Deauville Rally. This fantastic event for pre-war cars started with breakfast at the Eiffel Tower. A cross-country regularity rally then took us to Rally HQ at the magnificent Hotel Normandie in Deauville.

The following day comprised a race around the town of Deauville, with only a few straw bales tied to the lamp posts for safety. This was highly exciting on the damp roads and GOB was up against some tough opposition. Later that night at the Gala dinner Sue and I were amazed to be presented with a trophy for the best performance.

After attending numerous Alvis Owner Club events, including Midland Alvis Day, where GOB won a Concours award. I sold her to finance another project. GOB 260 is now in Germany and I would love to get her back.

Mike Ridley

Exhumed at last from the walled-up garage. (Mike Ridley)

Richard Jones stands by the car in the workshop. (Mike Ridley)

The nearside view of the finished car. (Mike Ridley)

ALVIS CARS IN COMPETITION

Car Details: 1933 Firefly; Registration No. CH 2804; Chassis No. 10839; Engine No. 10839; Body Maker – Cross & Ellis.

With a strong interest in cars when growing up, our vintage motoring passion was fuelled by a neighbouring car enthusiast. We had the opportunity to drive and travel in a wide selection of 1920s and '30s cars of all shapes and sizes.

We purchased the Firefly from Ron Wilson in September 1995. Ron and Bob Graham had enjoyed great success with this car in a variety of Australian Vintage Sports Car Club events and proved time and again that you didn't need to be the fastest to be successful; you needed to be consistent and have a good navigator. Always well presented, it was a pretty car with a competition history, and we jumped at the chance to own and enjoy it.

Maritta proved to be a very good navigator, which was fortunate for me, and so we set out to follow in Ron's footsteps, competing in any and every event we could. Navigation trials, hillclimbs, sprint events, time trials, we tried them all, and although we rarely won, especially at hillclimbs or sprints, we usually finished in the points.

I did have one very memorable Mt Tarrengower event when I won the annual Alvis Trophy. Two Alvis competed that year, and almost any Alvis there should have been quicker due to engine size and weight; however, the clutch failed in a supercharged 12/50 on the start line in its first run, thereby giving me the win! We also managed some success at the then '3 Hills' Trophy, which relied more on consistency than outright speed. The Firefly was always consistent and reliable.

For several years, persistence paid off, and we managed to win almost every VSCC trophy the car was eligible for. It is also a wonderful touring car, participating in many local and interstate rallies.

Although currently off the road for several years due to engine problems, a replacement engine and gearbox have been purchased and it should be back on the road and competing in the near future.

Dale and Maritta Parsell

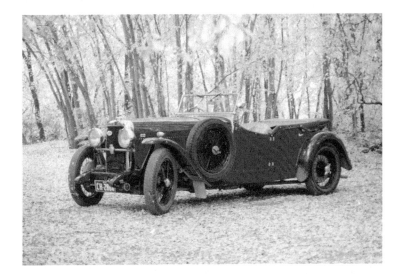

Alvis National Rally, Clare Valley, South Australia, in 1999 – a 1,000-mile round trip. (Dale Parsell)

At the Rob Roy Hillclimb, Victoria, in 1996. (Dale Parsell Collection)

At the VSCC Alpine Rally, Tasmania, in 1998. (Dale Parsell Collection)

ALVIS CARS IN COMPETITION

*Car Details: 1933 Firefly Special; Registration No. XJ 5148; Chassis No. 10226; Engine No. 4.3-14130;
Body Maker: Western Coachworks Ltd.*

In 2016, I asked our AOC Chairman, Brian Maile, if he knew an owner of a fast Alvis road/race Special who would consider to giving it a new home. Brian established contact with Chris Jackson, the current owner of this Alvis Firefly Special, Reg. No. XJ 5148, and gave me his details.

He told me he would sell it when his new Alvis Special project has been finished, and after a few months we met up at Mallory Park. Chris had raced XJ 5148 successfully and mentioned that, incidentally, he intended to sell the car. Chris told me that he had raced the car at all the principal circuits in England, such as Donington Park, Silverstone, Cadwell Park, Oulton Park and Mallory Park. He had also taken the car overseas and raced it and entered hillclimbs as well at Angoulême, Poitiers and Briac. At Donington in 2008, he had been part of the Alvis Team, finishing in second place.

I made a short test run in the racer's quarter and approximately two months later my wife and I picked up the Alvis in Nottingham. My wife said, 'It's always the same, after a short trip to GB, there follows a second one to pick up an Alvis!' It's true, I'm only interested in the Alvis. They are well constructed, with good performance and a pleasure to drive.

Originally, this Alvis Special was an Alvis SA 11.9 Firefly sports saloon, bodied by Cross & Ellis (No. 214) and registered 3 January 1933. It has passed through five owners throughout its life, according to the Log Book, before being consigned to the scrappers, from where the rolling chassis was rescued in the nick of time.

Probably in the 1980s, the first conversion into a hillclimb special was carried out by using the original and complete rolling chassis and an Alfa Romeo Spider 2.2 six-cylinder engine and gearbox. Chris Jackson, who bought the Special in 1990, described the homemade body as 'Ned Kelly look-a-like body armour', and as the picture shows it's true! Chris also said, 'It was the ultimate death machine, and had not been entered in competition, thank God he never got around to take it on a hill!'

When Chris completed the Special project, XJ 5148 had a two-seater sports Special body to his design crafted by Western Coachworks Ltd, powered by a 3.5-litre Speed 25 engine. XJ 5148 was raced by Chris regularly in the UK at VSCC events. In 2008 a 4.3-litre engine was fitted, which is still in place.

My first race outing with XJ 5148 was in 2017, at the Nürburgring. More than 100 enthusiasts with their pre-war race cars met up in the historic racer's quarter for three days, racing on the old track Nordschleife and the GP track, following the Le Mans start procedure.

It was an amazing experience for me. XJ 5148 has lots of power, good road holding and I am looking forward to the future races.

Frank Mertens

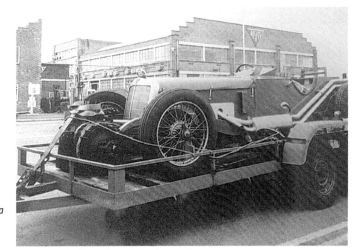

1990 – At the beginning, with an Alfa Romeo engine and 'Ned Kelly-style bodywork'. (Chris Jackson)

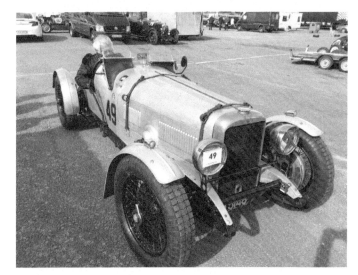

In the paddock at Silverstone as No. 49. (Frank Mertens Collection)

Nearside view in the paddock at Nürburgring. (Frank Mertens)

ALVIS CARS IN COMPETITION

Car Details: 1934 Firefly Type SB; Registration No. AXA 580; Chassis No. 11085; Engine No. 11539; Car No. 15919; Body No. 53546; Body Maker – Cross & Ellis.

The 1934 Firefly AXA 580 was first owned by David Goddard of Dulwich. I am the second registered owner since new, having acquired the car in 1986 from Goddard's family. The car had been badly stored for twenty-five years. After a long restoration project, the car's first outing was on a trip to Avignon, with a week of splendid motoring, wine and hospitality in the company of the late Peter Black at his Alvis Club de France annual meeting, never to be forgotten.

A fortuitous shunt by a tired lorry driver on the return trip in France led to an introduction to Rod Jolley and his company Solent Vintage Engineering. Body repairs and the total rebuilding of the engine and clutch, with many alterations and mechanical tweaks, resulted in a very competitive car. The Alvis Firefly model has long lived as the poor relation to its peers for many years, but AXA 580 has proved the pundits wrong.

Historic rally preparation in the '90s required the fitting of a Halda or Tripmaster, mechanical stop watches, good cockpit navigation lighting, including a 'potty' (a large magnifying glass illuminated in a large circular tube about 12 cm high, enabling map-reading in bad light and at night time). Nothing digital was allowed as I learnt early on when heavily penalised on a Monte event. I was grassed on by a Bentley driver for having a digital alarm clock pinned to the dashboard. This was probably to keep the navigator awake, but it cost us a Vintage victory. There were no singing or dancing digital electronics, as they allow now. Mechanical preparation involved an abundance of spares, fitting twin fuel pumps, coils and lighting to suit this type of event as well as an electric cooling fan. The original Firefly does not normally require a fan or water pump.

The 1996 LeJog (Land's End to John O'Groats Endurance Rally) was my first endurance event. Regardless of blowing a head gasket and burning out the electrical regulator at the start of the rally, it resulted in a class win and Spirit of the Rally Award. In the 1997 LeJog event, we were a part of the victorious Alvis Hares Team, alongside Mike Tomlin and Ken Burnett. Five Alvises started and five finished in an event far more arduous than the modern version; this was Alvis at their height in historic rallying! We were learning, and there were no mechanical problems.

Over the following twelve years, a series of European Historic Events with Philip Young's Classic Rally and Endurance Rally Organisation, HERO and other similar organisations, has allowed the Firefly to be competitive across Europe and the UK. The car's weight and poor turning circle have made for some frustration, especially in timed speed and mobility tests, but reliability, comfort and storage space has created a rally vehicle that few others can match. The delights of forest sections in Poland to flat-out blasts up the Turini or Stelvio, with snow chains knocking holes in the rear mudguards – all these events make for lifetime memories and friendships more important than the competition.

Summertime high-altitude routes have been our Achilles heel, with a combination of heat and rarefied air causing fuel vaporisation problems that regardless of heat barriers, or even in extreme conditions, removing the bonnet, have not totally resolved our problems. Firefly brakes, when a car is fully loaded, can leave a lot to be desired!

George Melville

At the Monte Carlo Challenge in 2001 – in front of Paul Carter in his Bentley. (Philippe Fugier)

Developing biceps on the many hairpins at the 11th Classic Marathon in 1999 in the Auvergne, France. (Phillipe Figier)

LeJog 1997, somewhere in the UK. (George Melville Collection)

ALVIS CARS IN COMPETITION

Car Details: 1934 Speed 20 SB; Registration No. XKP – 341; Chassis No. 11326; Engine No. 11776; Body Maker – Terdich Bros, Melbourne, Australia.

On 7 April 1934, the bare chassis was dispatched to R. J. Hancock, a Melbourne Alvis agent. The original owner, William Sear, Chairman or General Manager of Lever & Kitchen in Melbourne, and living at Gisbourne, 60 km north-west of Melbourne, used the car for his daily drive to the office.

Recorded owners start with David Bamford buying it from Tim Hewison, President of VSCC (Vic.), in 1960 for everyday use. A head coming off a valve damaged the piston, so the engine was reconditioned, sleeved to standard bore and the camshaft was rebuilt, ground to a higher performance level.

David collided with a VW van just weeks before he was to be married, but it was repaired in time for the honeymoon. Eventually the Alvis needed restoration, which David could not afford, so he reluctantly sold it to a prominent Alvis Club member, the late Andre Chaleyer, in about 1975.

After being told that oil pressure was unexplainably low, Andre went off to a rally and broke the crankshaft. It was caused by a main bearing cap becoming detached due to the bolts pulling out of the aluminium crankcase.

Melbourne architect/engineer Austin Tope, the next owner, was responsible for the restoration and had a lot of bodywork done by Richard Stanley, a recommended Victorian restorer. Austin kept meticulous records of all work done. Upon Austin's death the car went to an antique dealer in the Dandenongs, who indecently interferred with it, and sold it to crash repair and car collector Bernie Mack, who rarely used it during about three years of ownership.

I bought this car from Bernie in January 2008, at which point it was running like a 'hairy goat', but I could see its potential. It was found to have two bent pushrods, two bent carby needles and was hopelessly out of tune.

These problems were overcome, but a noise that I had assumed was just a noisy tappet proved to be a faulty cam. I tried to ignore this noise but after a couple of years I had the engine removed by a sports car specialist to have the camshaft reground. The bores were badly pitted by corrosion (laid up) so the engine had to be re-bored to the maximum and new valve guides and hardened seats were fitted. The Alvis has been running well, but initially there was a deep squeaking noise when the engine was under load. This remained undiagnosed and eventually disappeared.

I bought a 4.1 crown wheel and pinion from Red Triangle in the UK, replacing the 4.7. This has proved a big improvement for cruising (about 22 mph per 1,000 revs) and acceleration is still good. It is a great car and I love it, except for the brakes, which in spite of all my efforts are still unsatisfactory!

The body, made by Frank Terdich, is unique and rare. I met his grandson, Chris Terdich, at the Collingrove Vintage Hillclimb in 2015. He was most interested to inspect our Alvis as it is the only other Terdich body he has ever seen! The family emigrated from Croatia in the late 1800s.

Anne and I have taken part in four interstate National Alvis rallies and our car performed faultlessly.

Peter Mott

Resting under the trees near the RAAF Museum at Wagga Wagga, NSW, Australia. (Frances McDougall)

Driving in the hills on the 2011 Alvis National Rally. (Frances McDougall)

ALVIS CARS IN COMPETITION

Car Details: 1934 Speed 20; Registration No. AXV 325; Chassis No. 11171; Engine No. 11617; Car No. 15862; Body No. 3015; Body Maker – Vanden Plas.

An advert in 2008 for a Speed 20 VdP tourer in Portland, Oregon, resulted in an initial discussion, but in September 2009 we were at a family wedding in the US so I contacted Cameron Sheehan who told me, 'It's still here if you want it, come and get it!' On my return to Manhattan I had been more extravagant than my wife and younger daughter and their shopping!

Cars UK shipped it and retrieved the original registration, AXV 325. A very good friend had recommended a firm in Worcestershire that specialised in pre-war Astons, but who had just restored a 1934 Speed 20. Their advice was, 'Drive it and tell us what is wrong with it.' And that is exactly what I have done for seven years.

The first Flying Scotsman Rally in 2011 started at Brooklands and there were ten Alvises among the entries. Philip Young, the organiser of the Peking to Paris rallies, and his team at the Endurance Rally Association (ERA) had devised wonderful driving roads, tests and regularities for three days to Edinburgh.

In 2012 Red Triangle had produced new cranks and con rods for Speed 20s. This was a great opportunity that turned into a wonderful but expensive engine repair. The Flying Scotsman was completed with a loaned Model A Ford while AXV was in hospital! 'It got me from Peking to Paris so it should get you from London to Edinburgh!' said a most generous friend.

We entered our car in 2013 as No. 21, starting from Ware in Hertfordshire for Gleneagles in Auchterarder. My son Richard and I were to take it in turns to drive and navigate. We had fun and a big splash on our way to Gretna Green and Drumlanrig Castle among the splendid watering holes.

With four sons it was only right that each should have his turn, and 2014 was with Antony, who was alarmingly fast round cones. Unfortunately we took a shortcut and leapt off a 1-foot concrete base! This is where the assistance teams are such a wonder; all was straightened out and we just got maximum test penalties!

It was the lovely lakeside town of Annecy for the Alpine Trial of 2015 with my son Philip. One of the highlights was his drive of the Montvernier Staircase. This vertiginous road manages to compress seventeen hairpins in 2.4 km, and was used by the Tour de France for the very first time that year.

We entered the Flying Scotsman again for 2016 with my son Peter. Bless the Alvis for a roof; we had sun, rain and then snow – in April. The windscreen wipers kept us going and we finally arrived in glorious sunshine at Gleneagles.

14,000 miles in seven years have given us enormous Alvis fun.

Michael Joseph

A big splash on the 2013 Flying Scotsman with my son Richard Joseph. (Gerrard Brown)

Climbing after the hairpin on the Alpine Trial; lakes and sunshine with my son Philip in 2015. (Haase Photograph)

The finish at Gleneagles on the 2016 Flying Scotsman Rally. (Michael Joseph)

ALVIS CARS IN COMPETITION

Car Details: 1935/37 4.3 Sports Special Brutus; Registration No. EHP 99; Chassis No. 14651; Body Maker – Brian Strong.

Brutus was constructed in the late 1950s by Derek Strong. It was built as an off-set single-seater with an Alvis Speed 25 engine. The rear overhang of the chassis was cut and removed, and the rear suspension was modified to a quarter-elliptic arrangement.

Sometime later Sir John Venables-Llewellyn bought the motor car, fitted a 4.3 engine and opened the body up to qualify it as a sports car. Ownership then passed on to Jim Kennard in 1966. Jim was in business in Sherborne, Dorset, and was often seen 'bumbling' around the town in Brutus, which is where I set eyes on it.

I remember thinking to myself, 'What a fantastic car – I'd love to own that one day!' – never imagining for a moment that it would actually happen. The exhaust note, big wheels, polished aluminium body and the one aero screen were an inspiration for my young self as an apprentice panel beater.

Several years later, Peter Woodley purchased Brutus. It was during a conversation at Curborough in the spring of 1979 that I suggested that if he ever wished to part with the Alvis, he should call me. In October of that year, he did just that, and a few months later Brutus was mine. Peter had rebuilt the Alvis and claimed to me that it had 200 bhp at the wheels!

However, first gear was impossible to use on the start line, and indeed Jim Kennard had earned himself the nickname of 'Jumping Jim' due to the rear axle winding up, producing a hopping effect at the start of a race. I eventually added additional tramp bars to the rear suspension, which greatly improved the situation.

As the AOC Competition Secretary, I had the idea of staging an all-Alvis race and the 1985 VSCC April Silverstone was the event chosen. Unfortunately for me, the differential 'cried enough' on the start line and the race had to be halted – a nerve-wracking experience.

I managed to stop another race later that year at Oulton Park, and following that dramatic accident Brutus was totally rebuilt, with further modifications being made to the rear suspension. These alterations allowed first gear to be used in anger, vastly improving start line times. Now with a super straight chassis, set up on my Caroliner jig, Brutus drove and handled like never before and was resplendent, clothed as it was in a new Rod Jolley body, and returned to successful competition both here and on the Isle of Man.

I often thought that the accident improved the motor car, but unfortunately the same could not be said for me! In my opinion, Brutus was the epitome of what a competition car should be, and it provided me with an enormous amount of pleasure and success. In 1993, I decided to sell Brutus to Marc Hevia, a French surgeon, and I believe that it now resides in Germany.

During my ownership of twelve years, the car had been very active and consistently successful in all disciplines, including racing at Silverstone, Thruxton, Oulton Park, Castle Combe and Willaston Circuit on the Isle of Man; sprinting at Curborough, Colerne, North Weald, Carver Barracks, Weston-super-Mare and the Isle of Man; and hillclimbing at Prescott, Gurston Down, Shelsley Walsh, Wiscombe Park and the Isle of Man.

In long-distance relay races, such as the Six-Hour Relay held at Silverstone in 1980, Brutus completed 123 laps out of 251 for the AOC Team. In 1981 the AOC Team won first Pre-War and second overall and in 1984 Brutus completed ninety-three laps out of 222, with the AOC Team finishing third in handicap and first place in the Historic Class B.

Brutus was entered in ninety various competitive events between 1980 to 1992 and finished in first place thirty-five times, second place twelve times, third place twenty-three times, and fourth place fourteen times, and was probably the most consistent Alvis in competition during that period.

Brian Chant

BARC Meeting at Gurston Down Hillclimb in 1984. (Brian Chant Collection)

Over the crest to Signpost Corner during the 1990 Manx Classic, finishing third place in class. (Brian Chant Collection)

In the dry, turning right at St Ninnians Crossroads, on Glencrutchery Road, Willaston Circuit, Douglas, Isle of Man, during the 1991 Manx Classic; Brutus finished third place in class. (Island Photographhgraphic)

ALVIS CARS IN COMPETITION

Car Details: 1935 4.3 Special; Registration No. DUU 900; Chassis No. 18703; Engine No. 14804; Body Maker – Homemade.

DUU 900 was built by Ian Wolstenholm in the 1960s and I bought it in 1976 from Bruce Spollen. Somewhat tired, a year elapsed to sort out problems to race at the VSCC April Silverstone 1978. This resulted in two seasons passed with a class win at Shelsley Walsh, and an all-day drive for the AOC team in the Six-Hour Relay race at Donington due to a series of mishaps with other members of the team. The 'Driver of the Day' was awarded to David Roscoe, and the car held the circuit records for fastest Vintage and PVT lap. At this point the engine was overhauled; improving to 174 bhp at 4,000 revs with a set of close ratio gears installed gave a much higher third gear and greatly helped in circuit racing.

Throughout its life DUU ran on the original Bowden cable brakes but when Denis Jenkinson entered the car for the Weston-super-Mare Sprint, he did enquire when I proposed to fit brakes! After two visits to the Isle of Man in 1989 and 1991 for the Manx Classic, Sparrowhawk, Chant and Roscoe collected a few 'pots'. A full season on the hills and circuits caused a dropped valve at the Six-Hour Relay at Silverstone and a comprehensive rebuild of the engine. My good fortune is that John Hadwick, a local engineer, companion and race mechanic for many years, agreed to rebuild the engine in 1996. Due to the non-availability of new pistons, a series of short blocks were produced so we could use BMW pistons, shorter pushrods and a new Phoenix crank and rods were fitted. The cylinder head, CR 7.5:1, and the smaller carbs were retained. Although the bhp had only increased to 178, the motor would now happily rev to 4,500.

The power increased water temperature, we louvered the bonnet, ran on 50 per cent antifreeze fitted a Facet racing pump near the fuel tank producing a fine handling Alvis with a powerful and 'bulletproof' engine.

The rest of my ownership was a pleasure and without problems, and when I passed the car over to Brian Maile after twenty-three years, the success continued, with him ensuring that the reputation of DUU 900 increased year by year.

David Roscoe

I acquired DUU 900 in early 2000. I had been competing in a 12/50 (the MacJob Special) and had come to know David by meeting him at various events. David said it was time to give up racing and I could buy DUU from him at an advantageous price as he wanted the car to stay in the UK. As fate would have it I was drawn to compete alongside him at the VSCC Brooklands Sprint in October 1999. Just as the start light was to turn green, David turned to me and mouthed, 'You could own this car'. He disappeared into the distance, leaving me for dead. I thought that I must follow up on his offer and I agreed to visit him in Devon. After a very hairy demonstration run and test drive, the figure required was exactly the maximum price I had set myself, so a deal was done. Later, after the car was loaded on the trailer, David said, 'You'd better have these then', and proceeded to load a vast amount of spares into my tow car. David was a very generous man.

I had great fun for the next seven years, achieving various class wins and places. It was totally reliable, reflecting the care and attention that David had lavished on it prior to my ownership. It was not only a good speed competition car, but also a comfortable road car.

In 2005 I drove to Angoulême, France, to compete in the Circuit des Remparts race meeting with my good friend and fellow Alvis owner Peter Brown. We ferried from Portsmouth to Saint-Malo and drove to Angoulême, north of Bordeaux, with Bernie and Dave Mulvany's 12/60 Beetleback. We had to change the fabric drive coupling overnight, but didn't encounter any further problems for the rest of the trip.

Qualifying second on the grid behind Albert Sparrowhawk in pole position, I got alongside Albert at the start, but he had the line to the first corner and I knew that there was no way that the wily old racer was going to give me the corner, and this order remained until the end of the race. It was an Alvis clean sweep, with Albert first, me second and another 4.3 coming third.

In 2008 the opportunity arose for me to acquire a Historic Grand Prix car, and I sadly sold the car to a buyer in Scotland, enjoying success with the Grand Prix car in events in the following few years. I have often regretted selling DUU, but I now know that it was the correct decision as it allowed me to enter the world of Historic Grand Prix racing, which has given me immense pleasure for the past ten years or so.

Brian Maile

Above left: At VSCC Silverstone. (David Roscoe Collection)

Above right: Jenks (DSJ) in DUU at Weston-super-Mare. (David Roscoe)

Brian Maile finished in second place at Angoulême, France. (Peter Brown)

ALVIS CARS IN COMPETITION

Car Details: 1937 'Clink' Single Seater 4.3 Special; Ex-Registration No. ELY 2; Engine No. 14217; Body Maker – Homemade body modified from E-type ERA shell.

In 1953 Lt-Com. Clinkard set out to build 4.3 Racing Special. He used, as the basis for his design, a similar car built by Bill Goodwin just after the war using a supercharged 4.3 engine – the Goodwin Special.

The Clinkard Special was built in 1953 based on a chassis from a 1937 saloon (originally registered ELY 2) and Alvis 4.3 engine No. 14217. The chassis was tubular and the rear axle was originally from a Speed 20, but was later changed to a Salisbury differential with a DeDion tube arrangement.

Likewise, the brakes were cable (later changed to hydraulic), and the front suspension was independent with coil springs. A heavy-duty clutch linked to a Silver Crest gearbox. The engine was supercharged with a Villiers Mark IV, blowing at 12 psi and driven by ½-inch duplex chain from the crankshaft. The fuel mix was 50/35/15 Methanol, Benzole and Petrol. Fuel consumption was 4 miles per gallon.

The car weighed 18 cwt (910 kg) and was clad in an aluminium body, which was from an E-type body ERA that had been removed after only one race and lengthened by 1 foot to fit the Alvis. Clinkard campaigned the car on circuits, sprints and the hills from 1953 to 1979, followed by an overhaul, which removed the supercharger and rebuilt the engine with three 2-inch SU carburettors. There is no record of power output, blown or un-blown, but from my experience in the form I raced it, I would guess at around 150/160 un-blown, and clearly a lot more when supercharged.

I bought the car from Clinkard in 1981 and was thus only the second owner. Apart from a thorough service in the winter of 1981, no modifications were undertaken during my ownership. I raced the car through the 1982 and 1983 seasons, but, in comparison to the two-seater 4.3 Special I owned at the time, the single-seater was a disappointment.

Two factors became apparent at the first VSCC Vintage Silverstone; firstly, that the car was considerably down on power without the blower and, secondly, that the aged Dunlop racing tyres compromised handling, which is another way of saying that I spun twice during the meeting. The car always attracted a lot of attention in the paddock, but was not as quick as it looked or sounded. The car ran at Silverstone, Donington Park (where it was hit up the back, but not seriously) and was shared with Brian Chant at Colerne. It did not, however, feature very high up the results.

The Clinkard was good to drive and gave me no trouble in the two years I owned it, but a house move from the North to a flat in London, and having much less free time, meant that the decision was taken to stick with the sports 4.3 DUU 900 and pass on the Clinkard.

The car was sold at auction in October 1983 and is believed to have gone to Germany. It was briefly for sale in the USA and then rested in the Brooklands Museum, in a rather tired state. Latest reports say that it is currently in the hands of an enthusiast, who may be restoring it for competition.

David Roscoe

The beginning of it all. Left to right: Bill Goodwin, David Roscoe and Lt-Com. Brian 'Clink' Clinkard at Assington Farm, Essex. (David Roscoe Collection)

David Roscoe racing the 'Clink' 4.3 Special ahead of a Ferrari at Woodcote Corner, VSCC Silverstone 1982. (David Roscoe Collection)

David Roscoe on the inside line at Woodcote Corner at VSCC Silverstone in 1982; note the change of the helmet colour. (David Roscoe Collection)

ALVIS CARS IN COMPETITION

Car Details: 1938 12/70 Special SB 13.22; Registration No. FLA 105, ex- AOC Mem. No. 2841, 7499 and 8021 (UK), ex-WJ 84 (France), ex- FÜ J 1939 H and ex- SC Y 1938 H (Germany); Chassis No. 15531; Engine No. 16015; Body Maker – Unknown.

According to the Alvis Car Record it was built as car No. 19656 with a Mulliner saloon body No. 43072, and was 'Despatched to Messrs: George Hartwell Ltd of Bournemouth 30th August 1938'. Nothing is known about the history of FLA 105 (at least from my side) for a long time, but in 1986 FLA 105 was listed as a Special in the Alvis Owner Club 12/70 Register. During the 1970s, '80s and '90s the car changed ownership several times. During this period three different owners are known from the AOC Register: Dr Ian Outram, David Stogdale and Jeff Ody.

On 30 January 1996, Coys of Kensington sold the car by auction in London (Lot No. 36).

The auction catalogue describes it having been rebuilt with two-seater alloy sports coachwork in 1973 and some other mechanical overhauls, and mentions participations at Colerne (82 mph) and at Prescott (60 seconds).

I bought the car in 2004 from a trader in Germany, near the French border. For me it was a golden opportunity, because the car did suffer some damage after severe weather in the south of France and the flooding of the garage of the French ancestor, thus the car was affordable for me. Only a little work, mostly solving electrical issues, had to be done to get her on the road again.

In 2005 my Alvis achieved the approval for German MOT and classification as a historical vehicle. The car has been in regular use since then, from short trips into the near countryside, over a more than 1,000-mile tour in South England in 2009, to major tours into the European Alps in 2010 and 2016. I also enter a lot of historical events, mostly hillclimbs, but also race circuits: for example, the Hockenheim F1 circuit and the F1 and old 'North' circuit of Nürburgring.

During 2011 a severe engine breakdown occurred during a hillclimb with a broken crank. The engine was completely rebuilt with high compression pistons, a high performance cam and a nitrided crank. Below are some examples of events I joined in with my Alvis 12/70 Special:

2005: Bosch Boxberg Klassik at the Bosch car testing ground – second in class.
2006: Oldtimer Festival at Nürburgring – demonstration runs on GP circuit and North circuit.
2008: Vintage Nürburgring – demonstration runs on GP circuit and North circuit.
2009: Rossfeld Hillclimb in the German Alps.
2010: Langenburg Historic Hillclimb – second in class.
2010: Classic Grand Prix at Hockenheim F1 circuit – demonstration runs.
2011: Vintage Montlhéry – demonstration runs in the famous banked oval in France.
2011: Jochpass Memorial Hillclimb in the German Alps – engine breakdown (broken crank).
2012–2013: Complete rebuild of original engine.
2014: Jochpass Memorial Hillclimb in the German Alps.
2015: Grossglockner Grand Prix Hillclimb in Austria.

Jan Mutschler

I had just bought the car in the winter of 2004/05. The French registration is shown: 1939-WJ-84. (Jan Mutschler)

Right: Rossfeld Historic Hillclimb in the German Alps in 2009. (Jens Jensen)

Below: In the European Alps. (Jan Mutschler)

ALVIS CARS IN COMPETITION

Car Details: 1938 12/70 Special; Registration No. CAX 223; Chassis No. 15163; Engine No. 15647; Car No. 19123; Body Maker – Special by Duncan Fish.

I purchased the car as a very rusty and worn-out saloon on 13 October 1984 for the sum of £250 from a guy in Crawley. At the time I was rebuilding a 12/70 Mulliner Tourer and bought the car for spares. After being inspired and encouraged by Laurie Merriott and Mac Hulbert, who had both built 12/70 Specials, I started the build in August 1990.

It was a tight budget. The engine was rebuilt, and by fabricating frames and brackets I managed to reposition the engine 16 inches back and several inches lower. The steering and brake mechanisms were also modified.

The body was the hardest part, but I picked up a Beetleback-style body from an Alvis owner in Hereford, then made doors and a bonnet to fit. I initially ran the car with the original 1¼-inch SU downdraught carb with standard exhaust manifold. The first event entered was at Wiscombe in 2006, with my ambition being just to get to the top of the hill, which I did.

The development history of the car is that in 2007 I fitted twin 1½-inch carbs and an aluminium fuel tank, followed in 2008 by rebuilding the gearbox with a new synchro second gear. The head was modified in 2009 with long-reach plugs. Dunlop racing tyres and a lightened flywheel were fitted in 2010. The next area of development was the brakes, in 2011. I fitted hydraulic brakes, with new radius arms front and rear. In 2013 I built a new engine together with a Volumex Supercharger and a new crown wheel and pinion to 4.75:1 and then 4.55:1.

Here is a list of the time improvements from 2006 to present day, after supercharging: Curborough Sprint 50.32 seconds to 43.50; Wiscombe Park 67.83 seconds to 54.97; Loton Park 90.13 seconds to 74.49; Shelsley Walsh Hillclimb 54.96 seconds to 42.83; Prescott Hillclimb 57.79 seconds to 49.51; and Harewood Hill 97.12 seconds to 78.76. Fitting the supercharger took the bhp from 70 to 100.

The development of the car never really stops in terms of handling, with adjustments being made to suspension settings, springs, tyres and tyre pressures. In hindsight, I should have considered weight issues a bit more, and possibly should have shortened the chassis for better handling.

I'm satisfied with the engine performance. It has proved to be reliable and I don't intend to increase the supercharger boost, for fear of mechanical failure. The car is great fun to drive and its performance probably matches my age and driving ability.

Duncan Fish

Climbing the hill at Wiscombe Hillclimb in 2016. (Derek Webb)

Exiting the hairpin at Wiscombe Hillclimb in 2016. (Derek Webb)

The cooling system, the Volumex Supercharger and engine, 2013. (Duncan Fish)

ALVIS CARS IN COMPETITION

Car Details: 1940 12/70 Saloon; Registration No. GWJ 298; Chassis No. 15869; Engine No. 16354; Car No. 20328; Body Maker – Mulliners Body No. 43412.

I was going to buy a Riley Kestrel 12/4 but my brother Nicholas saw this car advertised. I went to have a look and, being more expensive and of better quality when new, I bought the car from John Sargeant, an AOC member who lived in Stoke-on-Trent, in May 1990.

My wife and I have owned it for nearly twenty-seven years and have competed in various VSCC rallies. When we bought it, I had Tim Abbott Engineering check the car over and make a few improvements to make it easier to run and drive.

We then entered it in the Measham Rally in 1991, where we finished after a very icy and cold rally in the Black Mountains in Wales. Having taken the car to marshal at the 1993 Buxton Rally, we entered the Buxton in 1994, where we finished but had a serious engine problem on the way home, which required an engine rebuild by Tim Abbott.

It took part in the Alvis 75th Anniversary celebrations in Coventry, also in 1994, where over 100 Alvises drove from the old factory site through Coventry, past the Mayor to the new factory near the M6. I then competed in the Measham Rally in 1997 with Lee Stanley as my navigator, and again finished the rally.

We did the RetroRun at Silverstone Classic in 2000, starting from Stowe School and ending at Silverstone, and the Alvis was chosen to be shown to Stirling Moss, who was involved with the sponsor, Footman James.

The car was present at the 2009 VSCC 75th Anniversary Rally celebrations in Malvern and was entered for one of the road runs. Finally, it did the Spring Rally in 2014 from the Bicester Heritage site. The car has been maintained by Abbott Engineering, and then a colleague who looked after our buses and vehicles in our mobile advertising business maintained our car with parts from Red Triangle. The car also had the front wings and running boards rebuilt and new springs installed front and rear, plus new kingpins by Red Triangle incorporated in 2001.

More recently, a fairly comprehensive overhaul was undertaken at Red Triangle in 2015, which included the cylinder head coming off, adding new guides and valves, and undertaking radiator repairs, as well as checking everything and renewing as needed since the engine rebuild in 1994.

William Lees

At the finish of the January 1971 VSCC Measham Rally at the hotel in Hereford; note the ice on the number plate. (William Lees)

Visiting the new Alvis factory after the tour through Coventry for the 75th Alvis Anniversary in April 1994. (William Lees)

At the finish of the VSCC Buxton (Northern) Rally in May 1994. (William Lees)

POST-WAR PERIOD:
1945 TO 1967

Car Details: 1954 TC21/100; Registration No. PGJ 3; Chassis No. 25627; Engine No. 25627; Body Maker – Mulliner.

In 1960 I needed a reliable car to tour the classic sites of Greece and Turkey. It had to be a saloon because of the security risk posed by a soft-top. When the Alvis TC21/100 was launched in 1954 I had decided it was the most desirable new car, so when searching the private car advertisements in the London Evening News I chanced upon one being sold by Mr C. A. Wale, I bought it.

So, it was in the summer of 1960 that I took my newly acquired Alvis TC21/100 over the potholed roads of the Balkans and Greece to Turkey, returning via Bulgaria. By the time I returned two exhaust valves had burnt out and the car was running on only four cylinders. But Alvis catered for owners who wished to do their own maintenance. The handbook included full instructions for dealing with such an issue and the Alvis tool roll contained the necessary spanners and feeler gauge. All I had to do was to telephone Alvis and within a couple of days I received the required parts plus an invoice requesting payment.

In 1963 I undertook a two-year tour with a British firm to work in Pakistan. Thus, in the summer of 1963 my wife and I drove PGJ 3 via Iran, crossing the Dasht-i-Lut (Salt Desert) and the Baluch Desert to Quetta in Pakistan, and on to Lahore. On arrival in Lahore I had new engine mounting brackets made by a gunsmith using steel twice the thickness of the failed originals plus a pair of 18-inch tyre levers. By repairing punctures (myself), I greatly reduced their incidence. I finally twigged that each repairer put a piece of gravel between the inner tube and tyre to give his brethren down the road further work. We used the Alvis to visit the hill stations plus for holidays in India, Kashmir and Afghanistan. In Pakistan the car had to be registered on Pakistani plates and insured in Pakistan, which also covered motoring in India. In Afghanistan there was no concept of motoring insurance.

During the spring of 1967 I took up the offer of a two-year tour in Iraq. Mindful of our experience of the 1965 Indo-Pakistani War, we resolved to take nothing of value – if a choice had to be made between evacuation and staying to look after our possessions, it was going to be the former. We drove PGJ 3 via Lebanon, Syria and Jordan to Iraq, where the car had to be registered on blue 'foreigner in Iraq' plates. Six weeks after our arrival war broke out with Israel. The UK ambassador advised us to join his armed convoy to Tehran, which I did using the Alvis. On returning to Iraq, and after the country became more stable, we used the Alvis to visit the important archaeological sites. During this time we also used the Alvis for holidays in Iran, Jordan and Kuwait. In Jordan we could use our Iraqi plates, but for Iran we reverted to our British registration. At the end of my tour we were unable to obtain visas to cross Syria, so we returned home in 1969 via Iran and Turkey.

For 1971 the Alvis was used in Greece, where I worked for a time, but after we moved to Cambridge in 1975 I needed a car for a daily commute, so PGJ 3 was then no longer our only car.

Ernest H. Taylor

Crossing the Baluch Desert between Iran and Pakistan in September 1963. (Ernest Taylor)

The Grey Lady before the India Gate, New Delhi, India, in the summer of 1964. The statue of King George V, which is visible under the canopy, was removed shortly after our visit. (Ernest Taylor)

The Grey Lady in front of the Grand Mosque (now destroyed) in Samarra, Iraq, in the spring of 1969. (Ernest Taylor)

ALVIS CARS IN COMPETITION

Car Details: 1958 TD 21 Prototype; Registration Nos 9 VMG and TI 11076; Chassis No. 25938; Engine No. 25938; Body No. 717/No. 18000; Body Maker – Graber Body/Park Ward.

There is quite a story behind this car. The chassis is a TC108/G originally earmarked for Willowbrook, which was switched over to Hermann Graber, a Swiss coachbuilder, in early 1958. The chassis was modified to accommodate a different gearbox and to give more leg room to the rear-seated occupants.

The lines of the body were somewhat muted from a previous Graber design of his own TC/108G. However, the car was fitted by Graber with a more refined nose, a newly styled and wider radiator grille, different front air intakes, a higher waistline and a different treatment of the rear.

The car was shipped to the UK and finished by Park Ward, as well as being used by this English coachbuilder, under instructions from Alvis themselves, as a 'template' for the production TD 21 model. Alas, the production cars were quite different in many areas.

In two years' time, the car was registered in the name of Park Ward Ltd. 9 VMG was used to test some different design improvements, such as front and rear disc brakes, an automatic gearbox and a fabric Webasto opening roof. All these modifications are still with the car today. At the time, the car was also used as personal transport by Mr Ward.

Its second keeper was Rolls-Royce Ltd, then a London impresario, followed by a Mr F. Ford, not connected to the US family. When I purchased it in 2011, it really took a lot of courage to start and then follow through this restoration.

I had fallen in love with this model as a boy, which to me represented the epitome of British motoring in the late '50s and early '60s. So the first 'competition' for 9 VMG was to try and vacuum-clean my bank account, and it almost managed to do so.

The car was entered in a few rallies and concours in England during 2013 and 2014, winning a number of well-earned prizes in the concours, but rallies are not really 9 VMG's cup of tea.

The car was then exported to Switzerland, where I live, and over the years it was entered in several more concours, mainly in Italy, Switzerland and France. It is now registered TI 11076.

I know this is a book about competition, but even in a concours there is quite a lot of competition. You have to present your car in superb condition, with all its story and evidence of what you assert, and with a lot of smiles for judges and for kids who leave marks all over the car.

Some competitions turn out well, with the car so far winning two Best of Show prizes and several first and second prizes. It is not so easy to win in Italy, the kingdom of the Ferrari, Alfa Romeo and Lancia, at a concours competition.

But as they say, make way for class and quality.

Giacomo Olivieri

Being canvassed (judged) at the Classic Club Italia Event at Cassolnovo, Italy, in 2015. (Giacomo Olivieri Collection)

On English plates (9 VMG) at Fougères Rally 2014. (Giacomo Olivieri – Lugano Cadro)

At the Coppa della Perugina, Perugia, Italy, in 2015. (Giacomo Olivieri – Lugano Cadro)

ALVIS CARS IN COMPETITION

Car Details: 1959 TD 21 Series I Saloon; Registration No. SVY 710; Chassis No. 26051; Engine No. 26051; Body No. 18072; Body Maker – Mulliner Park Ward.

The reason I decided to buy an Alvis is easily explained. When my father was still alive over fifty-five years ago, he had a friend just down the road called Ernie Smith, who, back in the '50s, bought an Alvis. I can't remember which model it was as it was so long ago, but my father was so impressed that he thought he must not allow himself to be upstaged by Ernie, and so he bought himself an Alvis too. I can't remember which model he bought either, but I am trying to find out the history of my father's Alvis through our Alvis Archive Trust.

In the end my father wound up with three in succession, the last of which was a Graber saloon. I was working in Africa when he died, so I flew back to help my mother and assist her in settling down again. My father was very happy-go-lucky and the last thing he bothered about was maintenance, so the Graber was rather a wreck, with the mechanics in very poor condition, and my mother and I decided it had to go. Since then I have been the opposite of my father, and I do try and take an interest in what goes on underneath the bonnet, even though tackling mechanical faults is nearly always beyond me unless they are very simple. It irritates me if I suspect something needs attention and I feel compelled to have the suspected fault put right and keep the Alvis properly maintained.

When I retired at the age of sixty-six I came back to Dorset, where I had spent my childhood, and bought a bungalow near the county town of Dorchester.

After about seven years or so I thought that, before I fall off my perch, I must try and emulate my father and buy an Alvis too. I joined the Alvis Owner Club and started looking around. In W. H. Smith, the newsagents, I saw among the motoring magazines a copy of Classics Weekly, which had an advert for a 1959 TD 21 owned by an Alvis enthusiast, Jack Clover, who lives in Norfolk. Jack had four Alvises at the time, and I soon found out that he is a highly respected member of the Alvis community in his part of the world, as well as a superb amateur engineer.

He brought it down to my bungalow on a trailer and gave me a test drive. I have now had it for about seven years and soon found myself in the Alvis community. There was a monthly meeting of Alvis owners about 35 miles from home, which was very interesting to attend, but most of us travelled a considerable distance to the pub where we had our meetings, so after a while some of us formed a similar group closer to where I live. This has now settled down to be a group of owners of various classic cars meeting monthly.

The South West branch of the Alvis Owner Club has regular meetings, which are a great pleasure to visit not only from the social point of view, but also from the places where we meet for rallies and social meetings.

The maintenance of my Alvis has presented considerable problems. It took me some time to find a good maintenance engineer and I found one in Brian Chrimes, who has his workshop not far from Coventry, where Alvis cars were manufactured until 1967. Brian has done a superb job for me as he has only worked on Alvis cars since he started as an apprentice with Red Triangle, who took over from the original Alvis company. I also have Mark Kirby, who runs his own garage and has owned two Alvises, and who is also a superb mechanic.

In all, at my advanced age, as I am now in my eighties, I find that owning my Alvis has brought me a great deal of pleasure.

John Wincey Prior

John Wincey Prior's TD 21 outside the church of Mudford, which is a delightful village near Yeovil, Somerset. (Helen Jones)

Offside view of John Wincey Prior's midnight blue TD 21 outside the cemetery of Mudford, Somerset. (Helen Jones)

This rear view shows off the graceful lines of the Mulliner Park Ward bodywork, with lowered rear wings – an attraction at car events. (Helen Jones)

ALVIS CARS IN COMPETITION

Car Details: 1964 TE 21 DHC Series III; Registration No. AUW 66 B; Chassis No. 27097; Engine No. 27097; Body Maker – Mulliner Park Ward (MPW).

I acquired the car in late 2015. It was only the second that I saw but as there were only a few on the market at the time, distance to view was a significant practical consideration. The car was with a long-standing classic dealer and came with quite a bit of history and some interesting ownership provenance.

The first owner was Sir Roger Fray Ormrod, one-time Lord Justice of Appeal and a Fellow of the Royal College of Physicians. He was often involved in cases where his dual qualifications were an asset. He was noted for ruling in 1970 that April Ashley (a famous pioneer subject of a male-to-female sex change) was 'not a woman for the purposes of marriage' and declared her marriage to the eldest son of Lord Rowallan void.

He owned the car for twenty years until it was acquired by Red Triangle in 1984, who in turn owned it until 1992. It featured in the August 1992 issue of Classic & Sports Car in an article on Red Triangle and their restoration services, being described as having been restored from a wreck and included as a showcase of their skills. At this point it changed colour from beige to metallic blue.

Subsequently sold by them, it had several owners until myself, including a City type involved in a financial scandal who 'fled' with the car to Monaco, where it lived for a while.

My time with the car has been a mixed bag. Shortly after my purchase I had a serious fall and was hospitalised with a ruptured knee, being left unable to drive for twelve weeks; fortunately it's an automatic, so I was able to drive 'Douglas Bader' style. He, of course, owned several Alvises, including a TE automatic that he apparently drove with his left leg over the transmission tunnel, so I adopted the same technique!

It has since been on many pub runs and to the Alvis International Weekend in 2016, and will be going again in 2017. Most Sundays there is a gathering of classic and other interesting cars in the neighbouring village, and the TE is a regular participant. Now that I am fully mobile again, it is hoped that this year it will also making appearances at the local Alvis Owner Club meets in the Anglia area. It particularly suits the longer distance events that would be a bit of a stretch in one of my pre-war Alvises.

It is essentially standard other than, having been restored by Red Triangle, with changes having been made to both body and to trim, all beautifully colour coordinated in blue. The hood is a cut above the standard vinyl offering and is made in lovely mohair with a West of England cloth headlining. Modern inertia reel seatbelts have also been fitted.

Following a starter issue, a high-torque starter has just been installed, which certainly enhances starting performance. Possible future changes may include a conversion to fuel injection for modern standards of performance and reliability (which is reversible, of course).

In conclusion; is this a competition car? Well, not quite, but it certainly is a stylish touring motor car with a sporting edge and four full-size seats – and the roof opens to enjoy good weather! Compared with earlier Alvis models, particularly the pre-war types, the suspension and handling are definitely boulevard cruiser, rather than sports car. The six-cylinder engine and auto gearbox are equally more suited to a relaxed style of driving, and combined with the power steering it makes for a comfortable long-distance driver.

Bryn Jones

Frontal view. (Bryn Jones)

Aerial front view. (Bryn Jones)

Offside rear view. (Bryn Jones)

ALVIS CARS IN COMPETITION

Car Details: 1964 TE 21 Saloon; Registration No. CLC 770 B; Chassis No. 27212; Engine No. 27212; Body Maker – Mulliner Park Ward.

My earliest memories revolve around vehicles, and like many boys from my generation I spent hours playing with toy cars. My father was a vicar, and whenever possible I would ask for a ride in one of his parishioners' cars if it was more upmarket than my dad's Morris.

This would usually be a Rover or similar, and I remember being taken to primary school every day in a friend's Daimler Conquest. British luxury saloons with a sporting edge quickly became my focus, and after studying Engineering at university I joined Jaguar Cars, which meant driving past the Alvis works in Coventry on my way to work at Browns Lane.

Alvis had stopped making cars by then, but was right in the centre of my area of interest due to its elegant restrained styling, leather and walnut interior and a sporting nature powered by a straight-six 3-litre petrol engine... Having decided I would own an Alvis one day, I had to wait until 2003 to be able to afford a suitable car, and so started my searching in earnest.

A lot of time was spent reading Alvis books, speaking to owners and looking at cars for sale at Classic Car shows, as well as joining the Alvis Owner Club. This helped me focus on specifics: a TD, TE or TF saloon with steel wheels, manual transmission, an original interior if possible and a colour to my liking. After eighteen months of looking at unsuitable cars, I finally found the right car with a classic car dealer; an additional point in the car's favour was the most complete service history I have ever seen.

After close inspection and a test drive the purchase was agreed, and because I had two young children, rear seatbelts were fitted at my request prior to delivery. The car was put to good use immediately, attending classic car events and also family days out. Over twelve years of ownership the car has never let me down, and is rigorously maintained. Only minor repairs have been needed until last year, when a new head gasket was required. I also took the precaution of renewing the corrosion protection underneath the car and in the closed body sections shortly after purchase.

My view is that regular use is crucial to maintaining reliability. I keep detailed records of cleaning and maintenance to ensure that the car stays in concours condition, using good-quality wax and spending plenty of time in keeping things as they should be.

Consequently, the car has not deteriorated over the years, and has won sixteen awards at concours competitions, generally at Alvis events, and most recently first prize for post- war saloons at the 2016 International Alvis Weekend. It is rewarding to know that others appreciate the car, and I am conscious that it is also a car to be used. The enjoyment for me comes from maintaining and driving it, as well as entering concours competitions with the car.

Jonathan Wankling

Concours standard – rear and offside view in the park. (Rob Rowe)

Concours standard – front and nearside view in the park. (Rob Rowe)

Driving on the road again. (Jonathan Wankling Collection)

ALVIS CARS IN COMPETITION

Car Details: 1965 TE 21 DHC; Registration No. EFH 200C; Chassis No. 27242; Engine No. 27242; Body No. 9577; Body Maker – Mulliner Park Ward.

My father used to drive a 3-litre Rover when I was a boy. When he was looking to replace it in 1967, I was keen that he bought one of the last Alvises – a TF 21 saloon. I was to be disappointed, however, as he bought a 3.5-litre Rover instead. Ten years later I nearly bought a second-hand automatic TD 21 DHC, but in the end settled for a distinctly ropey Aston Martin DB5 instead. I paid for it with an overdraft from NatWest, which didn't amuse my father. I put the Alvis, rather shamefully, to the back of my mind.

The DB5 was sold, and a better DB6 Vantage acquired, which I still have. But then in 1986 my wife inherited an estate in Scotland from her father's cousin, the redoubtable Marquesa de Torrehermosa. Behind the stables was her Alvis – a red TF 21 saloon!

Her TF 21 was the last of a line that the Marquesa had owned since she was a university student in the 1930s. Her father had offered to buy her a car, and she had wanted an Alfa Romeo. He insisted on a British car, and so began her long-term Alvis ownership.

Sadly, her TF 21, registration number EKY 40D, was not a runner. It was so rusty that the wheels wouldn't turn on the axles. I called Red Triangle, and asked how much they would charge to restore it. The amount was more than the car would be worth, so I sold the car to a man who wanted the interior.

A couple of years later, with a promotion at work to my name, the Alvis itch reasserted itself. I rang Red Triangle again. 'Well', they said, 'as it happens we have just completely rebuilt a TE 21 DHC for the 1989 National Exhibition Centre show in Birmingham. It is now for sale – would you be interested?'

No further hesitation ensued and EFH 200C became mine. It had everything I wanted: the stacked headlights, the ZF 5 speed gearbox, its original power steering and, of course, wire wheels. With fresh black paintwork and new grey leather, she was a true beauty.

We have been together now for twenty-seven years and 31,000 miles. I took her to Scotland, to continue the Marquesa's tradition, and we roamed the rugged West Highlands. Then, with small children in the back, we went to the south of France on holiday. We rallied to Land's End, visited Brooklands and finally settled in the Surrey hills.

Along the way she has won numerous concours awards: International Alvis Day; first prize in Novices Cup Concours at Duxford in 1991 and equal first at Polesden Lacey 2009; the winner of the 1995 Land's End Classic Trial and the Scottish Alvis Day; second place in the Post-War Convertibles Concours and at South East Alvis Day in both 2002 and 2009; and first place in the Post-War Concours. The trophies have piled up on my study mantelpiece. The most recent was at Rudyard Kipling's house last autumn, which was appropriate as he had been godfather to another cousin.

When it comes to touring, there remains no more comfortable or stylish way to travel than by Alvis. With the sun up and the roof down, it is unbeatable. The Marquesa managed fifty years of Alvis ownership, and I hope that I shall manage that too to make a combined century.

Mark Seligman

Relaxing in the driveway at home with the hood up. (Mark Seligman)

The front offside view with the hood down. (Mark Seligman)

Aerial view of rear passenger area and the instrument dashboard. (Mark Seligman)

ACKNOWLEDGEMENTS

The production of a book like this cannot be achieved by oneself; it is a team effort. I am grateful to all the contributors for their individual stories and images, both digital and photographic. Living in New Zealand, I needed a reliable contact in the UK who could be my confidant. Brian Maile, the Chairman for the Alvis Owner Club (AOC) in 2016, agreed to fill this role, which he accomplished admirably and with distinction. Later, in 2017, he had to pass this role on to someone else, and Charles Mackonochie, who is the AOC Specials Secretary, filled this position enthusiastically. With his professional approach, he made a difficult job easier for me.

I am grateful to John Fox, the AOC Archives Trustee, who recommended Amberley Publishing to me. At Amberley Publishing I am grateful to Nikki Embery, Connor Stait, Victoria Fletcher and Louis Archard for their constant professional support and guidance in producing and publishing this book to their expected high standards.

The following people arranged to publish advance notices inviting contributions for the book: John Lang, Editor of the AOC and Alvis Car Club of Victoria, Australia, who agreed to write the back cover text; Jennie Kindell of the Alvis Owner Club; Dave Salmon and Gill Batkin of the Vintage Sports-Car Club Limited; Ian Sykes of the Alvis Register Ltd; Frances Tweedy, Editor for the Alvis Car Club of New Zealand; and Heather Goldsmith, Editor for the Alvis Car Club, New South Wales, Australia.

There are two key people in New Zealand who have been at my side throughout this project offering their help, support, patience and tolerance – my wife, Val Taylor, and Paul Beck, in Mount Maunganui, who helped unravel computer teasers for me.

Every attempt has been made to seek permission for copyright material used in this book. However, if we have inadvertently used copyright material without permission or acknowledgement we apologise and we will make the necessary correction at the first opportunity.

ALVIS CAR CLUB CONTACTS

United Kingdom

Alvis Owner Club (UK) Membership: Colin and Anne Hall, 37 Worlds End Avenue, Quinton, Birmingham B32 1JF, England. E-mail: membership@alvisoc.org

Alvis Register (UK) Membership: John Urwin, Corn Bank House, Corn Bank, Netherton, Huddersfield, HD4 7DR, England. E-mail: membership@alvisregister.co.uk

The Vintage Sports-Car Club Limited, The Old Post Office, West Street, Chipping Norton, Oxfordshire, OX7 5EL, England. E-mail gill.batkin@vscc.co.uk

Australia

Alvis Car Club of Victoria (Inc), PO Box 129, Gisborne, Victoria, Australia. E-mail: jdmelang@bigpond.net.au

The Alvis Car Club NSW Inc. Membership: Joe Toms, 2/163, Booker Bay Road, Booker Bay, NSW 2257, Australia. E-mail: joetoms@gmail.com

New Zealand

The Alvis Car Club of New Zealand Inc. Membership: David Joblin, 34 Joblin Way, Ohauiti, Tauranga 3112, New Zealand. E-mail: dnjoblin@gmail.com

Holland

Alvis Owner Club Nederland, Membership: A. Hillebrand, Brouwersgracht 33H, 1015GB, Amsterdam, Holland. E-mail: secretaries@alvisocn.com, info@alvisocn.com

Coen W. H. van der Weiden, Weerriben 36, 1112 KM, Diemen, The Netherlands. Phone: +31-20-695-7774. E-mail: Alvis@chello.nl

North America

Alvis Owner Club of North America, Membership: Wayne Brooks, 140 Race Street, PO Box 46, Bainbridge, PA 17502, USA. Phone: +1-717-426-3842 E-mail: waynealvis@aol.com

Denmark

Peter Bering, Kragevigvej 17, Kragevig, DK-4720, Praesto, Denmark. Phone: +45-5599-6089. E-mail: pb@arkitektbering.dk

Sweden

Alvis Svenska, Registret, Kåre Nordlander, Varvsgränd 14, ltr 852 32 SUNDAVALL, Sweden. Phone: +46-70-51 077 32. E-mail: info@alvisregistret.se

Switzerland

Dieter Schaetti, Eichenweg 4 CH-8700 Kuesnacht, Switzerland. Phone: +41-449109347. E-mail: dieter.schaetti@schatti.ch

Stefano Mastropietro, Chemin du Rayon de Soleil 6 Nyon, Waadt CH-1260 NY. Phone: 0041-762-021260

Germany

Manfred Fleishmann, Stammheimer Strasse 12, 63472 Altenstadt, Germany. Phone: +49-6047-1280. E-mail: fleischmaenner@t-online.de

BIBLIOGRAPHY

Clarke, R. M., Alvis Gold Portfolio 1919 – 1967 *(Cobham: Brooklands Books Distribution Ltd, 1989).*

Day, K. R., The Alvis Car *(Lewis Cole & Co. Ltd, 1966, 1967, 1968, 1970 and 1974).*

Day, K., Alvis The Story of the Red Triangle *(Sparkford: Haynes, 1981, 1989, 1997 and 2008).*

Day, K. and Williams, J. P. (eds.), The Alvis Front-Wheel Drive Cars *(Manor Press, 2005).*

Fisher, S., The Alvis Firefly *(Nairobi: Simon Fisher, 1969 and 2007).*

Fletcher, M. and Newby, C., Alvis TA 14 50th Anniversary Collection, CD *(Blackburn: AOC, 1996).*

Fletcher, M. and Newby, C., The 50th Anniversary Collection – Alvis 3.0 Litre *(Blackburn: AOC, 2001).*

Fox, J., Alvis Cars 1946 to 1967: The Post-War Years *(Stroud: Amberley Publishing, 2016).*

Hull, P. and Johnson, N., The Vintage Alvis *(Macdonald & Co. (Publishers) Ltd, 1967, re-issued by David & Charles Ltd, 1974, and The Alvis Register Ltd, Midhurst, The Alvis Register, 1995).*

Hull, P., The Front-Wheel Drive Alvis *(Leatherhead: Profile Publications Ltd, 1967).*

Nicholson, T. R., The Alvis Speed Twenty and Speed Twenty-Five, 3½ and 4.3 Litre Models, *(Leatherhead: Profile Publications Ltd, 1966).*

Simpson, N., The Alvis Speed 20 *(Lavenham: Lavenham Press Limited, 2015).*

Walker, N., Alvis Speed Models in Detail *(Beaworthy: Herridge & Sons Ltd, 2001).*

Wheeley, J., Fifty Years of Alvis Enthusiasm *(Singapore: Press Concern, 2003, via AOC Website).*

Williams, J. P., Alvis: The Postwar Cars *(Croydon: Motor Racing Publications Ltd, 1993).*